The Gundel

Classic Recipes
and Modern Day Dishes

Kossuth Publishing

Content

Recipes
Cold starters

Hot starters

Soups

Fish

Poultry

Meat dishes

Desserts

Foreword

For me Gundel is...

... a little piece in which all the cultural and gastronomic colourfulness manifests what this country, our homeland represents for centuries. I still remember, very clearly the first dinner I had here. It wasn't a very very long time ago... in 1989, not long after my family decided to move back home. I was with my father and by the end of the evening it was no question that Gundel would be a fixed point in my life. I learned a lot about Hungarian gastronomy here. I had plenty of time and opportunities to learn because between 1996 and 2002 my work tied me to this area, and every week I visited the restaurant's 'little sister', Bagolyvár several times.

It was also clear that when I got married in 1997 the family chose Gundel, we asked them to provide the food and drinks for the event. Eilika, my wife and I ate through several tasty menus before we reached the wedding menu. Its most special part was probably the ice cream composition which was created to resemble a bowl of fruits.

I have a very good, personal relationship with the restaurant and the people who work here. I love their flavours – especially the goose liver and, as a practising chocolate addict, their chocolate desserts – and the old, peacetime, elegant and sophisticated atmosphere which is the unique feature of this restaurant.

As I can see Gundel believes in preserving traditions and passing them on – although innovation plays at least a same important part. This is what I try to pass on to my children, because these two things make the world go by the most.

I wish for us all that Gundel would be a significant point in Budapest's and the country's life for a long long time. This place to be one of our most important cultural and gastronomic messengers in the world. Because it represents our mutual success a little as well.

Dr. György Habsburg Ambassador

History of the
Gundel House

Gundel is not luxury. Gundel is quality.

The history of the Gundel dynasty is closely intertwined with the history of Hungarian gastronomy and Hungarian hospitality. Contemporaries of the founder included outstanding caterers, such as Sacher, Ritz, Escoffier, who also left their mark. Károly Gundel refined Hungarian cuisine and combined it with influences from an ever expanding world. He had an ingenious knack for applying modern gastronomic technology. His pioneering work placed Hungary on the world map of gastronomy. According to the *New York Times* the Gundel Restaurant set up at the 1939 World Fair in New York did more to enhance Hungary's reputation than a shipload of tourist brochures could have done.

The Gundel House survived the ravages of history: two world wars, various economic crises and the painful years of nationalisation. The restaurant is proud to carry on the best traditions of Károly Gundel who once said 'I do not really see myself as a restaurateur selling food and drinks for money, but rather as a real Hungarian style host looking after the guests who honoured his home.'

Károly Gundel also enriched gastronomic history. Similarly to the two world-famous Hungarian composers Kodály and Bartók, who collected Hungarian folk music in all parts of the Carpathian Basin inhabited by Hungarians, Gundel collected local food specialities.

Many well-known politicians, artists, writers and athletes were regular guests in Károly Gundel's restaurants: the Gellért, the Royal Hotel and the Gundel House itself. The chefs of the restaurants, just like Károly Gundel himself, took great pleasure in creating special dishes for their famous guests – dishes which were then named after the guests. This is how eggs 'Munkácsy' style, bouillon 'Újházi' style, bean soup 'Jókai' style and beefsteak 'Feszty' stlye came into existence.

Tradition and commitment – the keys to success

The internationally well-known 'Gundel dishes' are mostly the refined versions of traditional Hungarian cuisine, fine tuned to the Gundel taste. During the creation of the rib steak a là Gundel – as Károly Gundel wrote – he and his chefs experimented for months to find the perfect balance of fresh mushrooms and paprika. Another characteristic example of Gundel's art is the Zander fish 'Gundel' style which applies the techniques of French cuisine but gives the dish a Hungarian character. The Gundel pancake flavoured with a dash of rum, walnuts and raisins, served with chocolate sauce became the popular dessert of all elegant Central European restaurants. Károly Gundel wrote several books about catering and gastronomy. The *Art of Catering* and the *Little Hungarian Cookbook* were translated into English and German as well. These and his articles played an important role in making the author and Hungarian hospitality famous and successful.

The innovations of the new age

George Lang, famous American restaurateur, gastronomic writer and journalist and Ronald S. Lauder, the well-known businessman took over the Gundel restaurant in autumn 1991. The aim of the reconstruction carried out between November 1991 and May 1992 by Adam D. Tihany architect (New York) and Roth Imre Roth és Fiai Ltd. (Budapest) was to regain the original character and atmosphere of the restaurant.

We make more refined versions of the traditional Hungarian dishes, continue traditions brought back from the Central European aristocratic cuisine and prepare the special dishes from all over the world – and following thorough experiments and tasting trials we created a lighter Hungarian cuisine reducing the cholesterol and calorie level of the dishes: using less salt, spices, so the new Gundel meals are lighter then the earlier versions.

In July 2004 the owner of the majority of CP Holding (which controls Danubius Hotels Plc.), Sir Bernard Schreier became the new owner of Gundel but the restaurant remained an independent business enterprise on the market with its unique face. The new owner supported the reconstruction of the kitchen in 2008 which cost 1 million dollars – it took 4 months and was necessary since 1992. After the rebuilding, the kitchen went through a complete technological renewal and now it meets all the modern day requirements. These days the market is becoming more demanding that requires emphasis on the highest degree of quality, so that every guest would leave satisfied. The tasty food is important, and so is the ambience in which it is consumed. The milieu is also strongly determined by the staff and the service, because that makes us enjoy ourselves or not in a restaurant. That is why in the Gundel House guests can only meet really good experts and attentive waiters with a sense of humour.

In his epoch-making kitchen the founder created wonderful desserts and cakes as well, Gundel pancake, Somlói sponge cake and the famous Gundel cakes amongst other favourites. We also continue this tradition. In the Gundel Patisserie old, peacetime marvels are on offer, with 'granny's tarts' and French pastries as well. Of course all our products are made following the original recipes, using the best ingredients, in 'Gundel quality'. We also await our guests with appearance, service and warm welcome, according to the fame of the place. The Gundel Patisserie is located by the main entrance to the Budapest Zoo, and it can be approached both from the street and from the Zoo.

Acknowledgements and prizes

After the political changes in the 1990's the Gundel regained its the flagship role in the Hungarian gastronomy and was awarded many times – a few acknowledgements and prizes (amongst many others):

- Egon Ronay's Guide, 1995 – 'The best restaurant in Central Europe'
- Sidney Morning Herald, 1999 – '...one of the ten best restaurants in the world'
- Restaurant 2002 – 'Gundel is one of the 50 best restaurants in the world'
- Condé Nast, Traveller – Ristoranti del mondo 2006 – 'Gundel is one of the 10 best restaurants in the world'
- Budapest Business Journal
  Budapest Business Dining Award 2010
  The Restaurant Award – One of the Best Restaurant in Budapest 2011
  Fine Restaurant Award 2012, 2013
- Time Out 2010 – 'The best Sunday lunch in town'
- Hungarian Tourism Quality Award 2010–2013
- Best of Budapest Award
  Best Catering 2010
  Best Restaurant in Budapest 2011
  Best Outdoor Dining Restaurant 2010, 2011, 2012
  Best Iconic Place of Hungary 2011, 2012
  Best Hungarian Restaurant 2012
- Michelin Guide Recommended Restaurant 2006–2012
  Top Class Comfort and Pleasant Restaurant Category
- Hungarian Magyar Brands 2012 – 3rd prize

Gundel History

1879 János Gundel, the founder of the Gundel dynasty opens his first restaurant

1894 The Wampetics restaurant opens where Gundel restaurant stands today

1910 Károly, the son of János Gundel takes over the Wampetics restaurant

1939 Gundel becomes the official restaurant in the Hungarian Pavilion during the New York World Exhibition

1949 Gundel is taken over by the state

1991 The rebirth of Gundel: the restaurant is bought and renovated by George Lang and Ronald S. Lauder

1994 The centennial anniversary of the Gundel building

1995 Lanched by Gundel the Liget Republic, the alliance of the institutions of the City Park is formed

2000 Greeting the one millionth guest in Gundel

2001 Founding of the Gundel Arts Awards

2004 Gundel restaurant is bought by Danubius Hotels Plc.

2010 The centennial anniversary of the founding of Gundel restaurant

2010 Gábor Merczi starts to work as Executive Chef in Gundel

2012 Gundel Patisserie is opened next door to the restaurant

Celebrities who dined in Gundel

Albert II, Prince of Monaco • Angelina Jolie & Brad Pitt • Ban Ki-moon • Otto von Habsburg • Henri, Grand Duke of Luxemburg • Hillary Rodham Clinton • George Bush the Elder • Elisabeth II, Queen of Great Britain and Prince Philip, Duke of Edinburgh • Madonna • Michael Flatley • Michael Schumacher • Michel Platini • Placido Domingo • Sir Roger Moore • Rubens Barrichello • Sir Andrew Lloyd Webber • Sir Georg Solti • George Soros • Vladimir Putin • All Hungarian Presidents and Prime Ministers • And many others

Gábor Merczi Executive Chef

My family has been working in the catering industry but they were not pleased when I choose this profession. Still, I was admitted to a catering school, and after the first week I knew that I was in the right place. Gastronomy is a passion in my life I can not live without – and I do not want to either.

Since I became executive chef I can not cook as much as I would love to. Currently it is not my job. I have to manage the kitchen, do a lot of organising, keeping things together, setting the main guidelines for the kitchen and ensuring excellent quality. I like subtle things. When I cook at home for myself, I start with something simple. The main point is that I should enjoy what I am doing – that makes food taste really nice.

I am said to be a sanguine person and I am not the calm type. However, when I arrived to Gundel in 2010 I felt like I found my way home.

I really like when I can create something with my own hands. In this, I can fulfil myself. Of course to control a kitchen, you need something else: being systematic and composed. An executive chef has to know all about everything. When I arrived to Gundel the question was, if I could change the system to my mentality. First I was forcing things a little because I really wanted to prove myself. Then after the first results, the situation has changed a bit. As a 'boss' I set up clear rules: they are strict but clean-cut. And I demand things accordingly. Every restaurant has a 'taste'. I think the old Gundel had traditionally Hungarian (and not Hungarian-ish) cuisine, with many French features which were fashionable at the fin de siècle.

In this sense, we did not break away from the tradition but we are more adventurous and modern.

What makes me happy the most is that there are more and more guests and many returning guests. Gundel for me is not only a workplace but the past, present and future of Hungarian gastronomy. This is where I can realise my dreams. I think you have to be humble and committed to traditional Hungarian cuisine and towards the Gundel. I insist on using Hungarian ingredients and the flavours of traditional Hungarian cooking. I have many tasks and goals with this restaurant. I would like Gundel to be the restaurant of celebrations. We have the environment and the quality service to achieve that. The most important thing is to make people to realize that dining, celebrating a birthday is not luxury but achievable quality.

Gábor Merczi started his career in Hungary where he learned the basics of the profession. Later he continued abroad where he became acquainted with French and international cuisine. He developed into a top chef while working in the elegant restaurants of large cruise companies and luxury restaurants of hotels in London and Budapest. In 2010 he finally cast anchored at the Gundel House.

He looked up many old menus to find out who cooked what in the Gundel Restaurant in the past one hundred years, what earned the Gundel its outstanding reputation. He read everything he could find about Károly Gundel, the great gastronomic and catering genius. This helped him to familiarise himself and others too with the flavours of the old times, giving our guests a really authentic Gundel experience. Gábor Merczi has been awarded a Maître Rôtisseur title by the international gastronomic association Chaîne des Rôtisseurs in 2011.

Mihály Fabók Head sommelier

I have strong family connections to wine and grapes. I am from Mende, a town near Budapest. I still live here, and my grandfather used to have a little estate in the area. I was about 5-6 years old when he allowed me to help him with the harvesting and wine-pressing. These traditions are very important to me, when you can pass on a profession within the family. I also try to continue this tradition, and a few years ago I planted new vine on an acre on my grandfather's old estate.

The love of wine accompanied me throughout my whole life. One of my first, determining memories is when I used to be an altar boy, and I served the wine and the water while the priest was reciting the liturgy.

It also had a significant effect on my life when I read in an astonishingly interesting book about the master of the cupbearers in our King Stephen's court. I think learning is very important. For me it not only means studying wine but also learning about mineral waters also – you can create a unique harmony by mixing the right wine and mineral water.

When in 2010 we completely renewed the wine list in Gundel the main objective was that we should serve the best quality Hungarian wines under our labels to our guests. I am a head sommelier in Gundel for 12 years and with my experience, I can say that during my work (apart from the compulsory humbleness) the most important is that every day we should open the restaurant in a joyous way and stand by the tables loving our guests. Catering is not only about money. One of the beauties of this profession is for me that I know what the favourite wine of the returning guests is. Also through wine, I can make contact with people, who are grateful if their needs are catered for. It is a bit like a theatre: during dinner the restaurant is our stage, we are the performers, we aim to please our guests, and honestly enjoy the 'play' of meals and drinks.

In Gundel we aim to serve special wines, and we must know how to select well. It is an exciting, joyful and rewarding task to explore new wines and makers. So what would I ask for the next five years? Mostly that more guests would dine in Gundel, feel and share the Gundel experience.

Mihály Fabók travelled all around the world before coming to the Gundel House. He learnt his trade in many exciting places from Berlin to Tokyo, from Scandinavian ferries to American luxury cruisers. He has been to almost all important wine-growing regions in the world to learn as much as possible about wine and catering.

By winning the sommelier championship in three consecutive years, he became a sommelier champion for life.

He represents Hungary and Hungarian sommeliers in European and world championships. He is a certified sommelier of the International Sommelier Guild and a member of the Hungarian Sommelier Association.

He is inspired by the inseparable and complementary elements of wine and gastronomy.

Latinovits Bar

Andrássy Room

Queen Elisabeth Ballroom

Family Room

Eggs in Jelly 'Munkácsy' Style
The regular customers of Gundel always included many famous public figures. Mihály Munkácsy, one of the best-known Hungarian painters, was one of them. The founder of the Gundel dynasty created this starter in his honour, and this dish became a big favourite of his. A characteristic painting by the artist titled *New Recruits*, which he painted in Paris in 1877, hangs on the wall of the restaurant.

Cold starters

Gundel Salad

Green Asparagus with Garlic and Sour Cream

Csekonics Salad

Marinated Venison with Roast Beetroot

Chicken Mousse

Duck Rillettes with Dried Figs

Creamy Veal Pâté on Freshly Baked Bread

Pork Jelly

Eggs in Jelly 'Munkácsy' Style

Marinated Salmon with Potatoes
and Sour Cream

Trout 'Lohina' Style with Fresh Herbs

Foie Gras with Cold Hungarian Vegetable
Stew ('Lecsó')

Foie Gras with Golden Sultanas

1 Gundel Salad

This dish is made special by the new flavouring of the new age and the fact, that both of the favourite vegetables of Károly Gundel feature in it.

Serves 4

200 g mushrooms cleaned, trimmed and diced 10 × 10 mm • 200 g yellow bell peppers diced 10 × 10 mm • 200 g white asparagus scalded and sliced • 100 g green beans scalded, trimmed and cut into 20 mm pieces • 200 g tomatoes scalded, peeled, diced 10 × 10 mm • 200 g cucumber peeled, diced 10 × 10 mm • 1 Boston lettuce sliced • 10 g pasrley leaves chopped • 3 g salt • 1 g freshly ground white pepper • juice of 1 lemon • 10 ml balsamic vinegar • 10 ml apple vinegar • 10 g icing sugar • 20 ml rapeseed oil • 20 ml cold demi-glace sauce

Method

Marinate the mushrooms (see p. 190).

To peel the peppers, first fry them in oil or in the oven. After peeling off the softened skin cut out the seeds and chop up the peppers. Carefully peel the asparagus, trim 10–20mm from the bottom, scald and then cool them.

Trim the green beans to the same size as the asparagus and scald them in gently salted water. (It is important to cool it down right away in iced water.)

Mix the vegetables with the mushrooms thoroughly, season them, add the demi-glace sauce (see p. 189), and the salad is ready to serve.

♀ Recommended wine

Egri Napbor 2011 – St. Andrea
Very complex, fresh salad with many
flavours. Full bodied, complex but not
too old white wines are recommended,
matured in wooden barrels.

2 Green Asparagus with Garlic and Sour Cream

In spring asparagus is not to be missed – we love using both versions. Anyone can make this dish in 10 minutes, and success is guaranteed.

Serves 4

1000 g green asparagus • 3 g salt • 1 g freshly ground pepper • 30 g peeled, chopped garlic • 50 ml rapeseed oil • 300 ml sour cream • 50 g fresh coriander leaves

Method

Carefully peel the asparagus, trim 10–20mm from the bottom. (When it is completely fresh, no need to peel. To test the freshness, simply chew one asparagus raw.)

Put the asparagus into a pot large enough, pour water on the asparagus, add salt and bring it to boil. Boil it for 1 minute then using a skimmer lift the asparagus out of the water and immediately plunge into iced water and let it sit for 2 minutes.

For the cream, heat the rapeseed oil and cook the garlic to slightly golden brown and crispy, and let it sit in the oil to cool down. Slowly and evenly mix the garlic oil with the sour cream and season it. To serve, use the coriander leaves to add even more flavour to the cream.

Recommended wine

Kürti Zöldveltelini 2012 – Frigyes Bott

Fresh, green vegetables with characteristic, spicy
sauce. Traditionally it is accompanied with
Sauvignon Blanc, but we offer a full bodied,
characteristic Zöldveletlini.

3 Csekonics Salad

This dish has been featured on our menu for about half a century. Count Cserkonics was a pioneer in Hungarian horse-breeding, and he supplied beef for the Emperor's Court.

Serves 4

400 g boneless chicken breast • 3 g salt • 1 g freshly ground white pepper • 5 g Hungarian sweet paprika • 100 ml rapeseed oil • 120 g roasted shrimp or crayfish cooled and diced • 400 g tomatoes scalded and diced • 1 Boston lettuce sliced • 200 g mayonnaise • 1 g cayenne pepper • 1 g tarragon leaves chopped • 5 ml tarragon vinegar • 5 ml cold demi-glace sauce • 50 g lightly whipped cream

Method

Season the chicken, stir the paprika and the oil and spread over the breasts.

Fry each side of the breast in a pan for 2 minutes, then put it on a baking tray and bake it in a preheated oven on 160 Celsius degree for 12 minutes. Let the chicken rest for at least 10 minutes before cutting it up to dices.

Mix the chicken with the tomatoes and the shrimps in a bowl, add the tarragon and the cayenne pepper and then gently stir with the mayonnaise, the demi-glace sauce (see p. 189) and the tarragon vinegar. Before serving top it with the whipped cream and the Boston lettuce.

♟ Recommended wine

Paksi Siller 2012 – The wine of the city!
The roasted chicken breast and the crayfish
make this salad really special. It is very
harmonious in taste, colour and intensity
accompanied by an exciting Siller with nice
tannins and flavours of red berries.

4 Marinated Venison with Roast Beetroot

Apart from buying the perfect ingredients, we try to make everything here (bake bread, smoke fish and meat or making jams).

Serves 4

320 g venison rack filet • 400 g salt • 400 g sugar • 150 g ground pepper • 10 g thyme • 10 g basil • 10 g sage • 10 g parsley • 40 ml rapeseed oil • 400 g beetroot • 5 ml apple vinegar

Method

Marinate the venison filet in salt and sugar for 24 hours at room temperature. After marinating, rinse in cold water and dry.

Rub pepper and the finely chopped herbs into the meat with some olive oil and wrap tightly in foil. Leave it to dry for 2 hours at room temperature, then place it into the freezer.

Wash the beetroot and place into the oven, with the peel on, at 180 degrees Celsius and roast for 40 minutes (roasting time may vary according to the size of the beetroots). Peel and dice. Mix with the reduction of sugar and vinegar (see p. 190), adding salt, pepper and rapeseed oil.

Cut the venison into thin slices using a sharp knife and it is ready to serve.

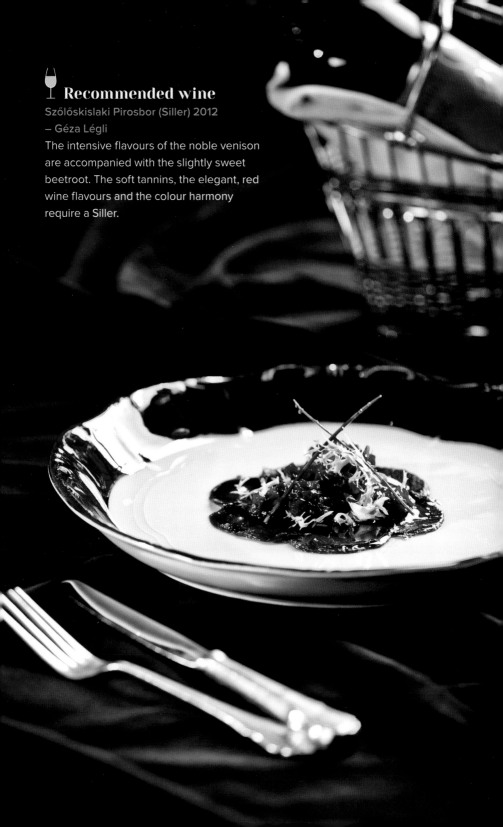

Recommended wine

Szőlőskislaki Pirosbor (Siller) 2012
— Géza Légli

The intensive flavours of the noble venison
are accompanied with the slightly sweet
beetroot. The soft tannins, the elegant, red
wine flavours and the colour harmony
require a Siller.

5 Chicken Mousse

It is an original French recipe from 1939 which we only brought out during a cookery course, because it became very popular. This is why it is featured in our seasonal, spring menu.

Serves 4

240 g chicken breast • 50 g carrots • 50 g celery • 50 g onions • 2 g salt • 2 g whole black pepper • 10 g parsley • 10 g thyme • 10 g rosemary • 30 g gelatine • 100 g mascarpone • 100 g whipped cream • 50 g salad mix • 2 egg whites

Method

Boil the chicken breasts in 600 ml bubbling water with the vegetables, salt, pepper and herbs.

Strain the chicken broth, mix it with gelatine and bring to the boil. Beat two egg whites and use 50 ml water to clarify the broth (see p. 189). Add the clarified broth to the cooking water and boil for 10 minutes. Remove from the heat and set aside for 15 minutes, then using a cloth, strain gently.

Purée the chicken breast with the carrots, then add in the mascarpone, the cream and 50 ml of the cooled but still fluid jelly.

For classical serving style, pour the mousse into molds lined with jelly (see p. 191). When it has solidified, dip the molds into hot water for a second to remove the mousse and serve.

An alternative option is to chop the mousse finely and serve with a tasty spring salad.

♟ Recommended wine

Móri Ezerjó 2012 – Csabi Miklós

Excellent, light meal enriched with vegetables and fresh herbs. We recommend Móri Ezerjó with light, fresh, lively tannins from the traditional Hungarian types, from one of the best makers.

6 Duck Rillettes with Dried Figs

Another classic dish. Duck is constantly on our menu, all year round. It represents the traditional flavours which one associates Gundel with all over the world.

Serves 4

500 g duck legs • 100 g onions • 10 g garlic • 500 g duck fat • 3 g salt • 2 g freshly ground black pepper • 1 g fresh marjoram • 1 g fresh chervil • 1 g dried hot peppers • 200 g dried figs • 100 ml red wine • 300 g milk loaf

Method

Coat the duck legs in salt, but only on the skin side. Leave to rest for 24 hours. Next day, start cooking them with the fat, onions and garlic. Cook slowly at 85 degrees Celsius until the meat comes off the bones – this should take about 4 hours – then take the duck legs and the vegetables out of the dish. Remove the skin and cut it into tiny pieces. Remove the duck meat from the bone and cut into large pieces across. Place the pieces of meat and the skin in a big bowl with chopped marjoram, chervil, salt, pepper, dried peppers and the onions fried in duck fat. Mix well.

Take an A4 size piece of aluminium foil and a piece of cling film the same size. Place the cling film on top of the aluminium foil. Place the duck mixture on the cling film and wrap up tightly into a sausage shape. After this, wrap the aluminium foil around the outside. Make sure the ends are sealed. Cool for at least 3 hours. Finally, unwrap the foil and slice the meat.

Soak half of the figs in cold water for approx. 3 hours, then chop to a purée. Cut the other half into small pieces. Meanwhile, reduce the red wine by boiling it to half the original quantity. As it reduces, add both the larger and smaller pieces of figs. Put aside when they are ready.

♆ Recommended wine

Villányi Portugieser 2012 – Gábor Szende
The duck is accompanied with the sweet, ripe,
fruity flavours of the dry figs and the red wine.
A more hearty dish in the beginning of the menu,
and it is best with a light and young, fruity red wine.

7 Creamy Veal Pâté on Freshly Baked Bread

It is also one of the classic Gundel dishes. We think it is very important to have a good pâté on the menu. With this we would like to show that hand made gastronomy plays an important part in our lives.

Serves 4

500 g veal shoulder • 100 g onions • 10 g garlic • 500 g butter • 2 g salt • 1 g freshly ground black pepper • 2 g fresh parsley leaves • 1 g fresh rosemary • 10 g chives • 500 g freshly baked bread • 100 ml brandy

Method

Cube the veal and start cooking it in butter. Add the onions, garlic and rosemary. Cook slowly (see p. 191), at **85** degrees Celsius, until the meat starts to crumble – it should take about 5 hours.

Take the meat and the vegetables out of the pan. Mince the meat, together with the vegetables, and mash the mixture through a sieve. Meanwhile, beat 150 g butter. Mix the minced meat and vegetables with the rum (which has previously been boiled to remove the alcohol). Next, add parsley, chives and freshly ground black pepper.

After this, mix the beaten butter into the pâté. Place in a deep bowl, make the top even and cool in the fridge.

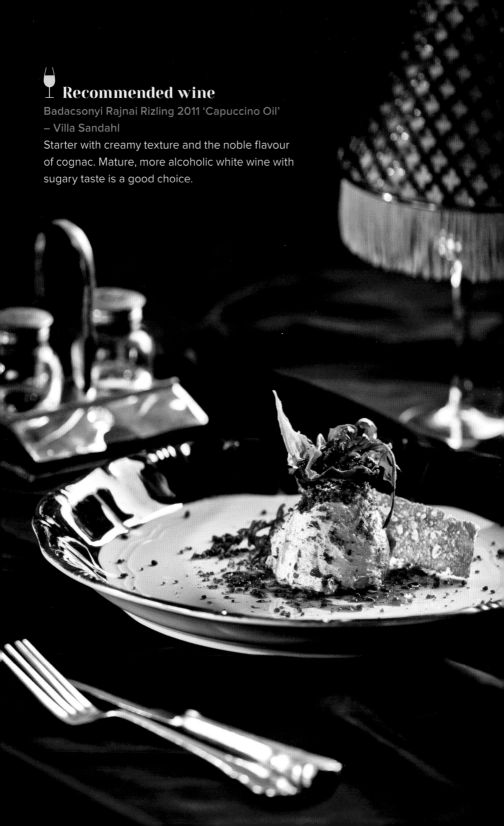

♟ Recommended wine

Badacsonyi Rajnai Rizling 2011 'Capuccino Oil'
– Villa Sandahl

Starter with creamy texture and the noble flavour
of cognac. Mature, more alcoholic white wine with
sugary taste is a good choice.

8 Pork Jelly

An original recipe from the Gundel cookbook from 1934.
We make it without changing anything, even today.
One of the favourites of the chef.

Serves 4

2500 g suckling pig, skin on • 150 g onions, cut in half • 5 g garlic •
100 g root parsley, chopped large • 200 g carrots, chopped large
• 100 g celery roots, chopped large • 2 bay leaves • 5 g paprika
• 5 g whole white pepper • 5 g salt • 20 g fresh herbs: thyme,
rosemary, marjoram, parsley • 4 l water • 4 egg whites, beaten
• 6 hard boiled eggs (boil for 7 minutes) • 100 g pickled gherkins

Method

Pour boiling water over the meat, then wash it in cold water.
   Put 4 litres of water in a 5 litre pot and place all the meat, vegetables, spices and herbs into it, including the paprika. Simmer on low heat until the meat is tender. While simmering, remove the foam from the top every 30 minutes, otherwise the jelly might end up cloudy.
   Once the meat and vegetables are tender, remove them gently from the pot, taking care not to break any ingredients. Leave them in a cool, airy place. Continue simmering the broth and let it thicken. When it has reduced to 2/3, clarify the broth (see p. 189) with the beaten egg whites.
   Pour the strained broth over the cooled meat and vegetables. When it has settled, keep in the fridge until serving. Serve with sliced hard boiled eggs and pickled gherkins.

🍷 Recommended wine

Somlói Juhfark 2009 – Tornai Cellar
Slightly sweet flavoured vegetables and
fine herbs make this dish more exciting.
Mature, full-bodied, white wines with slight
tannins play the leading role again.

9 Eggs in Jelly 'Munkácsy' Style

It is also an original Károly Gundel recipe which was used again after many years to strengthen our creed that roots are very important in gastronomy also.

Serves 4

4 eggs • 10 g salt • 20 ml apple vinegar • 160 g zander filet • 100 g tomatoes • 50 g celery • 50 g mushrooms • 10 g tarragon • 1 bay leaf • 3 g roughly ground pepper • 10 g salt • 80 g mayonnaise • 50 g icing sugar • 600 ml water • juice of 2 lemons, squeezed • 30 g parsley leaves finely chopped • 50 ml dry white wine • 15 sheets of gelatine • For clarifying: 2 egg whites

Method

Start boiling the stock with seasoning (salt, pepper, bay leaf). Cook the mushrooms and celery for the salad in the stock, alongside with the zander filet. Take the zander and the vegetables out of the stock and let them cool. Beat two egg whites with 50 ml water to clarify the soup (see p. 189).

Place the sheets of gelatine into water to soften for approx. 10 minutes, then add them to the warm stock and let it cool to room temperature – this is the way to make fish jelly.

Pour boiling water over the tomatoes and remove the seeds. Mix them with the finely diced celery, mushrooms, zander filet and add mayonnaise, finely chopped tarragon, salt, pepper and icing sugar to make a crunchy salad.

Poach the eggs in salt and vinegar water, then let them cool in icy water. If you wish to have runnier eggs, boil them for 4 minutes only.

Line the molds with jelly (see p. 190). Fill the dent with eggs and salad and let them solidify. Before serving, dip the molds into hot water to make it easier to remove the jelly and tip upside down.

Recommended wine

Lőczedombi Olaszrizling 2011 – István Jásdi
Classic starter with many vegetables and noble
fish from Lake Balaton. The mature, excellent,
white berry flavoured white wine we chose was
produced on the northern shore of the 'Hungarian
Sea', harvested from one of the best places.

10 Marinated Salmon with Potatoes and Sour Cream

In the past ten years salmon became an integral part of the menu in Gundel. It features in many variations: apart from marinating we prepare it smoked, stewed and grilled as well.

Serves 4

300 g fillet of salmon, skin on • 20 g salmon caviar • 200 g salt • 300 g sugar • 10 g freshly crushed black pepper • 20 g dill • chopped finely • 20 g parsley leaves chopped finely • 100 g butter • 150 ml sour cream • 400 g potatoes semi-cooked, coarsely grated • 20 ml smoky whisky

Method

Mix the salt and the sugar. Rub the freshly ground black pepper into the salmon. Place the fish into a dish large enough and then cover it in salt and sugar. Leave it in the fridge for 15 hours, then rinse gently in running cold water.

Place it on some paper towels and put the salmon back into the fridge to dry. When the surface of the fish is dry, rub whisky into it, and then repeat the same with dill and parsley leaves, too. (During the marinating, the salmon will lose a significant amount of moisture. This will make it redder in colour, harder in texture and stronger in flavour – it can no longer be considered raw fish).

Mix the coarsely grated potatoes with melted butter, parsley, salt and pepper, and fry them in hot butter until golden yellow. Form small potato pancakes from the mixture (not too thick, approx. 4 mm).

Serve warm.

♀ Recommended wine

Tokaji Furmint 2011
– Tokajicum / Gundel Selection
This dish features rich flavours; the smoky
whisky and dill play an important part.
The grapes are also excellent quality,
the best dry white wines are made from them
in Tokaj-Hegyalja. It was matured in a young
barrel and it is really full-bodied.

11 Trout 'Lohina' Style with Fresh Herbs

Another classic Gundel creation which can be the introductory dish for a celebration meal at Easter or Christmas.

Serves 4

4 pieces of trout fillets, skin on • juice of 1 lemon • 3 g salt • 30 g freshly chopped parsley leaves • 30 g leek sliced into thin rings • 5 g dill chopped • 5 g sage chopped • 1 Boston lettuce • 20 ml mayonnaise • 400 g cooked white or red skinned potatoes • 10 ml apple vinegar • 60 g sugar • 4 g salt and freshly ground white pepper • 50 ml rapeseed oil

Method

Place the trout fillets on a plate skinside down. Sprinkle with lemon, $1/3$ of the mixture of parsley leaves, sage and leek, salt and pepper. Fold it as seen on the photo, and with the use of a skimmer lift the fish onto a slightly oiled baking tray.

Bake the trout in a preheated oven (160 degree Celsius) for 6 minutes then let it sit to cool down to room temperature. Peel off the skin and trim the fillets so they are even and straight.

For the salad first boil the potatoes until tender, then peel off the skin and slice crosswise to 5 mm pieces.

Pour the water into a bowl, add the apple vinegar, the salt, the white pepper, the parsley leaves and the leek, stir it until the sugar dissolves then add the potatoes.

Before serving, make a salad out of the remained mixed herbs, and the Boston lettuce, and stir the sage and the dill into the mayonnaise.

♉ Recommended wine

Balatonszőlősi Sauvignon Blanc 2011
– Mihály Figula / Gundel Selection

The fish is made to be more exciting with fresh
vegetables and herbs. Our fresh Sauvignon Blanc
wine is full of grassy, herby, clearly felt fresh aromas.

12 Foie Gras with Cold Hungarian Vegetable Stew ('Lecsó')

The recipe is old, and the cooking procedure was slowed down as well to achieve more intensive flavours. The lecsó as a fresh ragout can accompany the liver really well.

Serves 4

800 g goose liver • 500 g goose fat • 3 g salt • 300 g green peppers diced finely • 300 g peeled tomatoes diced finely • 200 g onions chopped finely • 10 g paprika

Method

Soak the goose liver in icy water for 24 hours to remove any blood from the arteries. Heat the goose fat to 64 degrees Celsius and sauté the liver in it for 25 minutes on an extremely low heat. When the time is up, place the liver carefully on a flat plate and let it cool in the fridge for at least one day.

Heat goose fat in a hot pan, and fry the onions. When they have browned, add the peppers, and when they have also browned, sprinkle paprika on them. Stir, add the tomatoes in and then take dish off the heat after 1 minute. Transfer to a cold dish immediately. Let it cool for a bit, then store in the fridge until serving.

♆ Recommended wine

Szekszárdi Kadarka 2011 – János Eszterbauer
The characteristic and significant flavours of
the lecsó determine the choice of wine for this
dish. I recommend this wine because of its
light, ruby-red colour, subtle tannins and more
spicy style.

13 Foie Gras with Golden Sultanas

A recipe used many times. The dish constantly features on our menu for about 20 years. Preparing it at home it can be one of the highlights of a celebration menu.

Serves 4

400 g goose liver • 120 g golden raisins • 100 ml Tokaji wine • 100 g pointy red peppers ('kapia' type) • 5 ml apple vinegar • 120 g sugar • 6 g salt • 10 g roughly ground pepper

Method

Soak the goose liver in icy water overnight before cooking, then take it out of the water and let it warm up to room temperature.

Cook the golden sultanas in Tokaji wine until soft and strain. Continue to simmer the wine until it becomes as thick as oil and set aside till serving.

Remove the arteries from the liver when it is at room temperature. Place the livers in 10 mm thick pieces on a baking tray lined with foil. Season with a mixture of salt, pepper and sugar and pour wine over them. Place the golden sultanas in a row down the middle of the tray, setting a few aside for serving.

Lift the edges of the foil and fold it in half, using the foil to place the livers into a mold. Even out the top layer and fold the foil over the livers. After this, wrap the whole mold in another layer of foil. Place it into the fridge for 12 hours. When the time is up, steam it in the oven at 62 degrees Celsius for 22 minutes, squeeze the jus out, and then leave in the fridge for at least another 6 hours.

For kapia pepper chutney, bream the pergamen-like skin of the peppers, then wash them. Next, chop the flesh finely and boil slowly with the reduction of salt and vinegar (see p. 190), seasoned with salt and pepper, until it takes on the consistency of chutney. Let it cool.

To serve the pate, slice it with a thin bladed knife dipped in hot water. Use the reduction of wine and the pepper chutney to decorate the plates, then place the livers onto them, garnished with raisins.

Y Recommended wine

Tokaji Aszú 3 Puttonyos 2006 Sauska
– Gundel Selection
The flavours of Tokaji Aszú and the unique, creamy
taste of the goose liver provide a real gastronomic
experience. Our offer is a less sweet Aszú with
flavours of lively tannins, citrus, honey and raisins.

Santelli Royal

This creation of Károly Gundel was named after the great Italian fencing master who won a silver medal at the Paris Olympics in 1900 thanks to his unique technique nicknamed the 'Santelli style'. Italo Santelli was born in Italy and competed for Italy, but lived in Hungary for a long time after running into a controversy about a decision made at the 1924 Olympics by the Hungarian referee against the Italian team at a match between France and Italy, where Santelli supported the referee's decision. Santelli was a regular customer of Hotel Gellért in the 1930s.

Hot starters

Hungarian Style Asparagus

Vegetable Strudel with Baby Spinach Salad

Wild Mushrooms with Sour Cream

Filet of Zander Fish 'Carpathian' Style

Pancakes with Shrimp Filling

Sugar-pea Stew with Chicken Breast Meatballs

Santelli Royal

Pancake with Veal Stew

Eggs Benedict with Veal

14 Hungarian Style Asparagus

The Greek word for asparagus refers to the young shoots of the plant. The original recipe of this dish is also found in the Gundel cookbook from 1934.

Serves 4

1000 g asparagus (can be either green or white; should be fresh though) • 200 ml sour cream • 5 g paprika • 3 g salt • 3 g sugar • 30 g butter • 20 g breadcrumbs

Method

Clean the asparagus and cook in lightly salted, sugary water for 3 minutes. Butter an ovenproof dish. Use the remaining butter to brown the breadcrumbs and then mix them with sour cream. Use half of this sauce to line the bottom of the buttered dish.

Place all the cooked asparagus, dry if possible, on this layer of sauce. Pour the remaining sour cream over the asparagus and sprinkle with some breadcrumbs and paprika. Place in the hot oven and bake until the sauce thickens on top – it should take approx. 20 minutes. When baked, it is ready to serve.

Recommended wine

Villányi Rozé Cuvée 2012
– Vylyan / Gundel Selection

A light starter flavoured with a little paprika.
Rosé wines are very popular recently.
We recommend one with crispy tannins
and fresh, fruity flavours of red berries.

15 Vegetable Strudel with Baby Spinach Salad

One of the favourite dishes of the new age. It could be a dish for every day. In our restaurant it is featured on the seasonal menu.

Serves 10

Strudel pastry: **500 g (strudel) flour** • **50 g butter (not margarine), warmed up** • **500 ml water** • **20 ml vinegar** • **1 egg** • **3 g salt** • **10 ml sour cream** • **50 ml rapeseed oil** • Filling: **2000 g mixed spring vegetables** • **3 g salt, freshly ground white pepper** • Baby spinach salad: **300 g or 3 packs of baby spinach** • **20 ml mayonnaise** • **100 ml sour cream** • **50 ml mustard**

Method

First, mix lukewarm water with salt and vinegar. Start mixing the flour with the egg and butter – the texture of the pastry should be similar to thick dumplings. Beat it for at least 20 minutes to make it homogenous. When it is beaten, pour oil over it, then let it settle for half an hour on the cooker at room temperature, covered with a warm dish. To roll it, cover the table with a tablecloth and sprinkle strudel flour over it. Place the dough in the middle and roll slowly, pulling each side to the edges of the table. It should stretch easily, but once it starts to dry it will break, so do this quickly.

When it is rolled, add the filling, making sure it is distributed evenly, and sprinkle a little rapeseed oil over it. Use the table cloth to aid rolling up the filled pastry. Place in the oiled baking tray and spread oil with sour cream on top of the strudel. Preheat the oven to 180 degrees and bake for approx. 25 minutes, till golden brown.

Peel and grate the vegetables, fry until crunchy and let them cool. Do not add salt and pepper at this point, only season the vegetables when you fill the pastry!

Put 50 g baby spinach with all the other ingredients in a blender. Blend into a thick sauce. Cool and before serving, mix half of the sauce with all the remaining spinach. Serve the other half with the strudel, on the side.

🍷 Recommended wine

Balatonlellei Loliense white 2012 – János Konyári
Fresh spring vegetables in a strudel coating
with a young wine from the southern shore of
Lake Balaton, in which there are excellent ratios,
fine green fruity flavours, ripe fruits and long
aftertaste.

16 Wild Mushrooms with Sour Cream

It is the only dish on our menu in which mushrooms play the leading part. It is one of our seasonal offers.

Serves 4

100 g porcini mushrooms • 100 g morel mushrooms • 100 g chanterelles • 100 g sheathed woodtufts • 100 g oyster mushrooms • 50 g butter • 150 g sour cream • 10 g paprika • 20 g parsley leaves • 30 g onions • 300 g rye bread • cream

Method

Peel the mushrooms and dice into 10 x 10 mm pieces, except for the porcini mushrooms which should be set aside till serving.

Brown the finely chopped onions on butter, then add paprika and continue frying. Add the mushrooms and fry it all together for 1 minute, before pouring the cream over the vegetables.

Bring it to the boil.

For serving, mix the thinly sliced porcini mushrooms into the mixture and spread thickly on freshly sliced rye bread. Sprinkle generously with chopped parsley leaves to finish.

♟ Recommended wine

Egri Örökké 2011 – St. Andrea
Dish carrying the intensive
flavours of noble mushrooms.
Choose a full bodied, complex
white wine matured in oak barrels
for a longer period.

17 Filet of Zander Fish 'Carpathian' Style

We are very proud that this dish features on our menu all year round. It is one of the successful dishes of spring which our guests love as well.

Serves 4

720 g filet of zander cut into 4 equal parts • 50 g potato flour • 300 g shrimps • 200 g butter • 200 ml cream • 200 g oyster mushrooms • 500 g potatoes peeled, diced 10 x 10 mm • juice of 1 lemon, squeezed • 300 g parsley leaves chopped finely • 10 g dill chopped finely • 3 g salt • 2 g freshly ground white pepper • 20 ml brandy

Method

Salt the zander filets and coat them in potato flour, then fry on both sides in butter in a hot pan and set aside.

Pre-cook the oyster mushrooms, too. Simmer the potatoes slowly in cream until soft, adding salt only at the very end, and set aside until serving. Place the fish in the oven at 160 degrees for 6 minutes after setting an oyster mushroom on top of each piece of fish.

Meanwhile, reduce cream in a frying pan. When it has reduced to half the quantity, add shrimps and season with brandy, salt and sugar. Add dill at the end. When the ragout is ready, add cold butter to it. Next, heat the potatoes up, mixing parsley glazed with butter to them, and whisk. The dish is now ready to serve.

🍷 Recommended wine

Etyeki Pinot Noir Rozé Habzóbor 2012
– Kertész Cellar

Its unique taste is given by the shrimps, the oyster
mushrooms and the cognac. One of the recently
more popular rosé sparking wines, made from the
best ingredients, can be an interesting choice.

18 Pancakes with Shrimp Filling

Another classic Gundel creation. We chose this simple dish when we were looking for new recipes for our menu. It was changed a little: the lime and the coriander complete the sweet flavours of the shrimps.

Serves 4

Pancake mix: 200 g flour • 2 eggs • 2 egg yolks • 5 g icing sugar • 2 g salt • 200 ml milk • 200 ml water • 100 g rapeseed oil • Shrimp filling: 200 g shrimp • 100 g leek • 100 ml béchamel sauce (see p. 186) • 10 g fresh coriander • Juice of 1 lime • Nantua sauce: 200 ml béchamel sauce • 100 g shrimp butter (Beurre de Homard: see p. 186) • 100 ml cream • 1 g salt

Method

For the pancake mix all the ingredients until smooth. Let the pancake mix rest for at least an hour. Fry in an iron pan on medium heat, making thick or thin pancakes according to taste.

Stir the cubed shrimp into the heated béchamel sauce mixed with finely chopped leek. Add coriander and lime juice for flavour.

For the Nantua sauce boil the béchamel sauce with shrimp butter. When it has boiled, add a little salt.

To serve, make small parcels of pancakes stuffed with the shrimp filling and pour hot Nantua sauce on top.

♟ Recommended wine

Gundel Prestige Brut 2005 – Gundel Selection
Interesting starter with citrus flavours.
A dry champagne made with the traditional
methods can enhance the uniqueness, aromas
and fine tannins of the dish.

19 Sugar-pea Stew with Chicken Breast Meatballs

Stew is a traditional Hungarian 'genre'. Sweet-pea is the first sign of the summer, an all time classic!

Serves 4

400 g sugar-peas • 50 g potatoes peeled, sliced thin • 100 g leeks chopped finely • 30 g parsley leaves chopped finely • 10 g fresh coriander chopped finely • 200 g minced chicken breast • 200 g bread rolls soaked in milk • 200 ml milk • 50 g butter • 3 g salt • 1 g freshly ground pepper • 5 g paprika

Method

First, start boiling half of the sugar-peas in milk with the potatoes and half of the leeks. When cooked, use a mixer to purée it and then start cooking the other half of the peas in the purée. Simmer on a slow heat until the peas are soft. In the meantime, mix the meat with the soaked bread rolls thoroughly in a bowl. Season with salt, pepper, paprika, chopped fresh coriander and leek.

Next, form 8 equal sized meatballs from the mixture and pre-cook in a hot pan, then place in the oven at 160 degrees Celsius and roast for 6 minutes, till done. While roasting the meatballs, finish the pea stew by adding cold butter in small pieces to make it creamier, and finally add all the parsley leaves.

It is now ready to be served.

Recommended wine

Balatonfüredi Zenit 2012 (semi-dry)
– Mihály Figula

Fresh, young, bit sweet flavours with chicken
breast. The best choice among the white
wines is the youngest, fresh version with
a bit of leftover sugar.

20 Santelli Royal

The recipe is the original, the method although follows the guidelines of modern gastronomy. There is always a place for this course amongst the twenty traditional dishes on our menu.

Serves 6

100 g Hungarian style dry sausage, diced finely • 40 g tomatoes peeled, diced finely • 100 g spring onions sliced thinly • 5 eggs • 200 ml cream • 150 g green peppers diced finely • 150 g semi-hard cheese diced finely • 100 g lettuce leaves (any type) • Juice of 1 lemon • 10 ml rapeseed oil • Cottage cheese cups: 140 g cottage cheese or quark • 110 g flour • 100 g butter • 1 g salt • 1 egg yolk

Method

To make the cottage cheese cups, put all the ingredients into a bowl and mix thoroughly. Cool for approx. 60 minutes, and then roll to 3 mm thickness. Cut suitably sized circles out of the dough to line muffin molds with. Once the molds have been lined with the pastry mixture, place dried beans on top of the layer of dough in order to keep the shape during baking.

Bake in the oven at 160 degrees Celsius for 15 minutes. When the pastry cups are done, remove from the molds to cool and dry.

Prepare the filling: mix the cream with the whole eggs and set aside. Use a pan to fry the vegetables with the sausages, then cool them. Mix the cream and eggs with the fried vegetables and use it to fill the pastry cups. Sprinkle cheese on top and bake in the oven at 120 degrees for 20 minutes. Serve with fresh lettuce leaves.

Recommended wine

Villányi Siller 2012 – Sauska

It is a heartier, heavier omelette, especially because of the sausages. It requires a bit heavier wine than rosé, so we chose a bottle of Siller.

21 Pancake with Veal Stew

Most people know this dish as Hortobágyi pancake. Our version is unique because it is not too complicated, but made with the best ingredients.

Serves 4

300 g veal shanks • 100 g finely chopped onions • 10 g ground paprika • 40 g peeled tomatoes, seeds removed, diced 10 × 10 mm • 40 g green peppers diced 10 × 10 mm • 1 hot pepper • 100 ml meatstock (see p. 190) **• 100 ml sour cream • 100 ml cream • 100 g duck fat • 3 g salt • 1 g freshly ground white pepper • 4** pancakes (see p. 162)

Method

Fry the veal with the onions on duck fat, then remove the pan from the heat and add the ground paprika. Then return to the heat, fry it on low heat and add the tomatoes and the green pepper. Cover and let it simmer on low heat (for about 120 minutes). Pour in some of the stock if necessary, if the veal is not juicy enough.

When the veal is tender remove it from the paprika sauce, put it aside and purée the paprika sauce with a mixer. Mix the sour cream and the cream with a whisk in a mixing bowl then pour it into the paprika sauce. Add salt according to taste then put it aside until serving.

Cut the cooked veal into really small cubes, and mix it in a mixing bowl with a small amount of the paprika sauce, 2 tablespoons of sour cream, 2 g ground paprika, salt, pepper and hot paprika (according to taste) – it should be like gravy, not liquid. Boil the ingredients together in a pan. Then fill the pancakes with it and prepare for serving.

Recommended wine

Szekszárdi Fuxli Siller 2012 – Zoltán Heimann

A more heartier, heavier starter, based on a dreamy stew. Keep the red wines for the main courses, so we chose a well-known Siller with red wine features.

22 Eggs Benedict with Veal

A modern version of a classical dish. It is simple, and if we are after traditional flavours, it is a perfect choice, for example for lunch.

Serves 4

12 eggs (whole) • 500 g veal shanks • 200 g veal bone • 60 g butter • 60 ml sour cream • 150 g white bread • 30 g onions • 10 g duck fat • 2 g salt • 3 g paprika • 20 g fresh peeled tomatoes

Method

Chop the veal into pea-sized cubes and make a stew.

Veal stew: First, cube the onions and fry in oil. Add the paprika and the meat, and let it simmer slowly in its own gravy. If the gravy evaporates, add a little meat stock (see p. 190) as necessary. When the meat is half-cooked, add the tomatoes (chopped into small pieces) and cook until the meat is done.

Paprika sauce: It should be prepared in a similar way to the stew, but using meat and/or trimmings. When cooked, remove all bones and purée it. Add sour cream.

Eggs Benedict: Heat the water to 90 degrees Celsius with salt and vinegar. Carefully crush the eggs into the water and boil for 4 minutes. Rinse and cut the edges off.

Toast with butter: Slice bread and butter it on both sides. Fry in a hot pan until brown.

 Recommended wine

Szekszárdi Zweigelt 2011 – Gábor Merfelsz
The paprika sauce and the tomatoes give the
determining direction. A light, spicy red wine would
not disappoint us with its colours and aromas.

'Palóc' soup
The writer and MP, Kálmán Mikszáth,
who is often referred to as the Great
Palóc, asked János Gundel to make him
a dish that would be characteristic of
the region where the Palóc people
live and their cuisine. János Gundel
managed several restaurants during
his carreer. Wherever he went, his
regular customers followed him.
Mikszáth was one of them.

Soups

Cream of Watercress Soup

Cream of Leek Soup with Jumbo King Prawns

Cream of Asparagus Soup with Truffle Oil

Chicken Soup 'Újházy' Style

Gundel Crayfish Soup

Gundel Goulash Soup

Gundel Fish Soup

Roe Soup

Cream of Potato and Artichoke Soup
    with Smoked Beef Tongue

'Palóc' Soup

Cream of Porcini Mushroom Soup
    with Smoked Beef Tongue

Tokaji Wine Soup

23 Cream of Watercress Soup

Watercress sounds like a rarity, this long-forgotten vegetable can be used in many ways, and its flavours are quite strong.

Serves 6

300 g watercress • 200 g potatoes • 100 g leeks • 150 g sour cream (20% fat) • 100 ml cream (30% fat) • 500 ml water • 100 g butter • 2 g salt • 2 g freshly ground white pepper • heat proof blender or mixer

Method

Peel and chop the vegetables. Use half of the butter to start frying them. Do not fry too long, as they do not need to be cooked at this stage. Remove the watercress leaves from the stalks and add the chopped stalks to the frying vegetables. After 3-4 minutes, add all the water and bring to the boil. When it has boiled, continue simmering on the lowest heat possible, until the potatoes and leeks are tender. When all the vegetables are cooked, use the blender to purée the soup. As soon as it is smooth, add the sour cream and the other half of the butter to continue blending it. Finally, add the watercress leaves and blend again. The soup is ready when it takes on a nice green colour.

    Put a small watercress leaf in the bowls and serve the hot soup over this. Decorate with a little whipped cream on top.

 **Recommended wine**

Kürti Zöldveltelini 2012 – Frigyes Bott
Light, refreshing creamy soup with vegetables
and the distinctive aroma of the watercress.
This wine has green fruity features and its
tannins enhance its aromas.

24 Cream of Leek Soup with Jumbo King Prawns

One of the popular dishes of the new age. A very good example for the combination of simple flavours, which can create fantastic harmony.

Serves 4

100 g butter • 70 g onions chopped • 100 g leeks sliced thinly • 200 g potatoes peeled, sliced thinly • 50 g ginger peeled, grated • 400 ml stock • 180 ml cream • 6 jumbo king prawns • 15 g parsley leaves chopped

Method

Heat half of the butter in a large pot. Add the onions, leeks and potatoes, and steam until tender. Add the ginger and steam for a further 2 minutes. Stir occasionally. Pour in the stock, bring it to the boil, cook it for another 15 minutes, until the potatoes are tender.

Next, use a mixer to purée the soup base, adding the cream in gradually. After that, mix the butter in slowly, in small bits, stirring continuously until the texture is thick and creamy.

Peel the prawns, bring a little soup to the boil and throw the prawns into it. When it starts boiling again, take it off the heat and set aside for 3 minutes. Serve immediately, sprinkling the fresh parsley leaves on top.

 ## Recommended wine

Csopaki Cseszegi Fűszeres 2012 – István Jásdi
Creamy soup with prawns and ginger for the real
gourmands. A more fragrant, young white wine
with lively tannins can be a good choice to start
with this soup.

25 Cream of Asparagus Soup with Truffle Oil

One of the well-loved soups of spring. Fresh, simple dish and the truffle enhances the soft flavours of the asparagus.

Serves 6

1000 g white asparagus • 200 g potatoes sliced thin • 20 g celery roots sliced thin • 100 g leeks sliced thin • 400 ml asparagus stock • 100 g butter • 100 ml cream • 2 ml truffle oil • 2 g salt • 1 g freshly ground white pepper

Method

Use a peeler to strip the asparagus (the average asparagus is 220 mm long, the loss is approx. 30%). Chop the bottom 5 mm off the peeled asparagus, and then starting from the heads, cut a 40 mm piece off each piece. These are going to be added to the soup at the end. Chop the rest of the asparagus into extremely small parts and set aside.

Do not throw the peel away but use it to make asparagus stock. Put the asparagus peel into 500 ml boiling water, then remove from the heat immediately, cover and set aside to cool. When the broth has cooled, strain. Boil the other vegetables in the stock until they are tender. Add the chopped asparagus, and when it is also tender, use a mixer to purée it until creamy, seasoning with salt and pepper. Finish off by adding the cream, followed directly by the butter which should be added in small pieces. Use the mixer to whip the soup.

Before serving, pour hot water onto the asparagus heads and cut them in half. Place them into the soup bowls and ladle the hot soup over them. Add a few drops of truffle oil to the dish before serving.

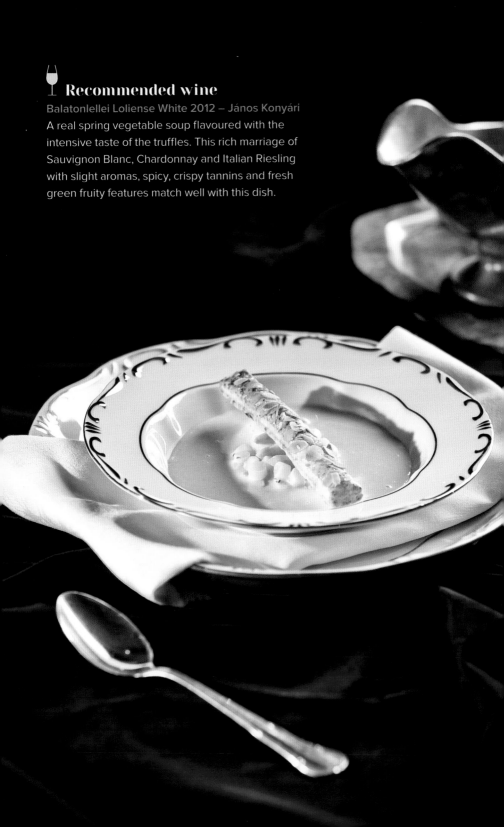

Recommended wine

Balatonlellei Loliense White 2012 – János Konyári
A real spring vegetable soup flavoured with the
intensive taste of the truffles. This rich marriage of
Sauvignon Blanc, Chardonnay and Italian Riesling
with slight aromas, spicy, crispy tannins and fresh
green fruity features match well with this dish.

26 Chicken Soup 'Újházy' Style

This dish is very well-known in Hungary. It is always on the menu on weddings and banquettes.

Serves 6

1 whole chicken (2000 g approx) • 200 g celery roots chopped • 200 g carrots chopped • 100 g root parsley chopped • 100 g oyster mushrooms chopped • 2 g black pepper • 10 g parsley leaves • 10 g fresh ginger • 2 g salt • 200 g vermicelli noodles • 1500 ml water

Method

First, clean the chicken thoroughly, wash, cut up and then pour boiling water over it. Rinse in cold water again and then start boiling in 1500 ml cold water. When the broth has come to the boil, remove the foam and continue simmering slowly. When the chicken is half cooked, add the vegetables. Season with salt and continue cooking with the vegetables.

   Wrap the spices and herbs into a small piece of canvas, knot it tightly and add to the soup while cooking. Continue until the meat is completely tender. Boil the noodles separately in hot salty water and add to the soup just before serving.

🍷 **Recommended wine**

Balatonszőlősi Sauvignon Blanc 2011
– Mihály Figula / Gundel Selection

A complex soup connected to our restaurant
with the essences of the vegetables and the
chicken. The choice is our Sauvignon Blanc
with its green fruity flavours, fresh tannins
– a perfect example of its kind.

27 Gundel Crayfish Soup

The original recipe lacks the fennel and Pernod, but with these two ingredients this classic dish was transformed to a really exciting meal.

Serves 4

500 g crayfish • 50 g butter • 80 g carrots, peeled and sliced • 60 g root parsley, peeled and sliced • 100 g leeks • 1 cherry tomatoes, cut into half • 4 g Hungarian sweet paprika • 100 ml cream • 400 ml crayfish stock (made from crayfish shells) • 50 ml Pernod or brandy • fennel, sliced thin

Method

Remove the crayfish shells and make stock from them: boil 450 ml water in a pot, while frying the vegetables and the crayfish shells on a little butter in another pan. When they are cooked, pour the boiling water over them, cover and let it sit for 60 minutes. After that, drain.

Put butter into a 4 l pot and fry the chopped vegetables for 5-6 minutes, stirring constantly. Add the tomatoes and the onions and fry for a further 3-4 minutes. Sprinkle paprika and flour over them, then pour the stock into the pot. Add white wine and the puréed crayfish shells. Simmer for 1 hour on medium heat, stirring occasionally. Use a strainer to separate the broth and transfer it into a 2 l pot.

Before serving, boil again with cream and fennel, and add Pernod for flavour.

♀ Recommended wine

Neszmélyi Álom Cuvée 2009
– Hilltop Neszmély / Gundel Selection
A more spicy, fragrant crayfish soup which
requires a full bodied, more complex, heavier
white wine. The choice is one of our most
excellent marriage of Tramini and Sauvignon
Blanc with fragrant, citrus-flavoured white wine.

28 Gundel Goulash Soup

A classic dish with traditional flavours which can 'summarise' the whole menu. In our restaurant it is made more special with the home baked bread.

Serves 6

200 g beef diced • **50 g onions, chopped** • **3 g Hungarian sweet paprika** • **50 g green peppers seeded and chopped** • **1 g freshly ground caraway** • **2 g garlic, crushed** • **100 g potatoes diced 20 × 20 mm** • **30 g tomatoes, diced** • **800 ml** meat stock (see p. 190) • **2 g salt** • **6 portion of** Hungarian dumplings (see p. 190) • **1200 g fresh** home-made Gundel bread (see p. 189)

Method

First wash the meat thoroughly then chop it to 2 cm dices. Sauté the chopped onions until golden, season it, add the paprika and the meat, fry it and fill it up with 500 ml of the meat stock.

When the meet is turning tender add the potato, the green peppers, the caraway, the garlic and the tomatoes, and fill it up with the rest of the meat stock. Simmer and cook until the beef and the potatoes are completely tender. Remove the fat from the surface with a spoon, add the dumplings, cook for about 5 minutes then let is cool of and sit.

Serve it with thin slices of hot pepper and fresh bread.

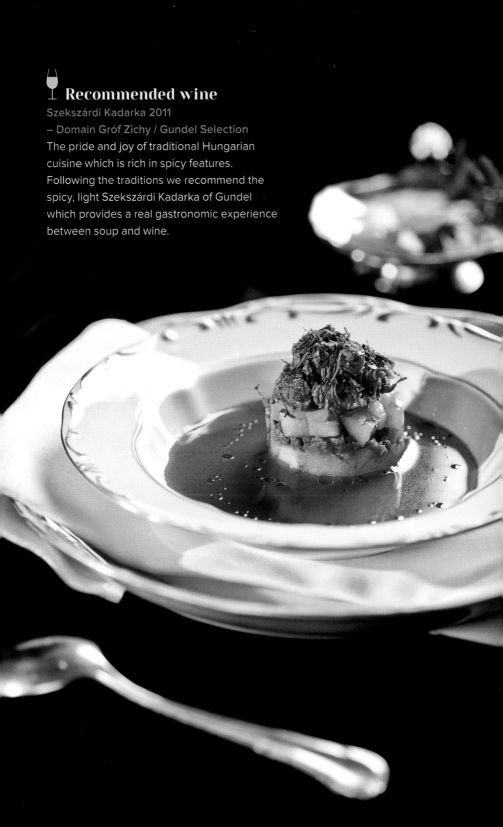

♈ Recommended wine

Szekszárdi Kadarka 2011
– Domain Gróf Zichy / Gundel Selection
The pride and joy of traditional Hungarian
cuisine which is rich in spicy features.
Following the traditions we recommend the
spicy, light Szekszárdi Kadarka of Gundel
which provides a real gastronomic experience
between soup and wine.

29 Gundel Fish Soup

The traditional fish soup is really good if it is made of three-four different types of fish. In our restaurant a separate chef controls the making of perfect soups.

Serves 4

240 g carp fillet • **500 g** carp bones • **200 g** catfish fillet diced 20 × 20 mm • **200 g** catfish bones • **200 g** zander fillet diced 20 × 20 mm • **200 g** fish chitterlings • **200 g** sliced onions • **10 g** garlic • **200 g** paprika (cut in half) • **50 g** tomatoes • **10 g** ground paprika • **10 g** hot paprika (thin slices) • **3 g** salt • **100 g** boiled dumplings (see p. 189) • **1200 g** home-made Gundel bread (see page 189)

Method

Put the fish heads and bones into a suitable size pot and make fish stock as follows:

Boil the fish bones with 1500 ml water, remove the foam after boiling and cook it on low heat. Add the onions, garlic, two types of paprika, tomatoes, 50 g ground paprika and a little salt.

After more then half of the water evaporated (after 1 hour) pour it through a sieve (squeeze the paste) – and your broth is ready.

In a 3 litres pot boil the broth slowly, for about 5 minutes with the three types of fish fillets and the chitterlings.

The vermicelli noodles should be made following the recipe but instead of boiling it in the fish soup, boil it in hot water, and put it into the fish soup only before serving. Serve it with fresh Gundel bread and hot paprika.

♛ Recommended wine

Szekszárdi Kadarka 2011 – János Eszterbauer
A Siller can be a good choice for the paprika
flavoured fish soup, but a light, spicy Kadarka can
make the food-wine harmony more unforgettable.

30 **Roe Soup**

It was one of the dishes during the 'Dinner Competition' in 1934. A real classic, which shows how high the gastronomic traditions were between the two world wars in Hungary.

Serves 4

300 g carp with heads • 300 g catfish • 50 g roe • 50 g milt • 100 g carrots, sliced thinly • 50 g root parsley, sliced thinly • 20 g parsley leaves, chopped finely • 20 g celery roots, chopped finely • 50 g onions, chopped finely • 10 g paprika • 2 g salt • 1 g freshly ground white pepper • juice of 1 lemon, squeezed • 1 bay leaf • 100 ml sour cream • 20 g butter • 10 g flour • 200 g bread rolls cut into strips, toasted in the oven for 12 minutes at 160 degrees Celsius

Method

Make fish stock (see p. 189) out of the fish and the bones.

Fry all the ingredients without oil, but only use half of the vegetables. Add cold water and sprinkle paprika on top. When the stock has boiled, turn the heat down and simmer for 30 minutes, then take it off the heat and set aside. If the stock settles, strain it with a sieve. After this, start boiling the stock again with the other half of the vegetables. Mix the flour with the butter and add to the slowly simmering soup in small bits (beurre manié, see p. 186). Boil for a while. After approx. 35 minutes add the roe and milt, stir the sour cream into the soup and serve immediately.

Sprinkle freshly cut parsley on top and serve with the toasted croutons.

🍷 **Recommended wine**

Csopaki Olaszrizling 2011
– Mihály Figula / Gundel Selection
A hearty, slightly spicy soup made with many
vegetables. We can try a full bodied white
wine from Lake Balaton, especially one which
is more characteristic, has strong tannins and
matured in oak barrels.

31 Cream of Potato and Artichoke Soup with Smoked Beef Tongue

The artichoke gives the determining flavours. In our restaurant we aim to use the chitterlings in a sophisticated style as well – this is a perfect example of that.

Serves 4

100 g leeks • 300 g potatoes • 100 g celery roots • 300 g artichokes • 500 ml meat stock (see p. 190) • 100 g cream • 2 g salt • 1 g freshly ground white pepper • 100 g smoked beef tongue • 50 g Craterellus mushrooms ('horns of plenty') • 100 g butter • juice of 1 lemon, squeezed

Method

Steam the vegetables with butter, and season with salt and pepper.
　Add the chicken stock and simmer for 40 minutes on low heat. When all the ingredients are soft, purée the soup and boil for a further 2 minutes. When it has boiled, gently mix the cream in.
　Add salt, pepper and lemon juice for flavour. Put aside until serving. Chop the smoked beef tongue and mushrooms julienne and add to the soup.

♆ Recommended wine

Egri Chardonnay Battonage 2011
– Nimród Kovács
Superb creamy soup flavoured with Cratellerus
mushrooms and smoked veal tongue. The winner
is a sensual Egri Chardonnay with smoky aromas,
creamy flavours with a slight hint of mushrooms.

32 'Palóc' Soup

Another original Gundel recipe. One of the rare dishes which we still continue to follow without any changes, because it really works in today's modern world as well.

Serves 6

600 g shoulder of mutton, diced 15 x 15 mm • 300 g onions chopped finely • 250 ml sour cream • 50 g duck fat • 100 g flour • 20 g paprika • 250 g green beans, chopped finely • 150 g potatoes, diced 15 x 15 mm • 1 g bay leaf • 2 g caraway • 1 g fried garlic • 2 g fresh dill chopped finely • 4 g salt • 600 ml meat stock (see p. 190)

Method

Fry the onions in a little fat, then add the washed, diced meat (15 x 15 mm) with paprika, ground caraway seeds and bay leaves, and sauté until tender. Boil the potatoes and the green beans separately in the meat stock, and when the meat has browned, add the vegetables and the stock to it. Season with salt.

Mix the sour cream with 100 g flour and add it to the soup before serving. Sprinkle a little finely chopped dill in your soup, too. If you like, add some fried garlic as a finishing touch.

🍷 Recommended wine

Szekszárdi Fuxli Siller 2012 – Zoltán Heimann

The soup which was created in honour of the famous writer, Kálmán Mikszáth is very exciting because of the tasty mutton. In this case we can choose a good Hungarian Siller with its soft, red wine features and silky tannins.

33 Cream of Porcini Mushroom Soup with Smoked Beef Tongue

The elegant, high life Gundel version of the classic mushroom soup. The smoked beef tongue makes it more characteristic.

Serves 4

200 g potatoes, peeled, sliced • 300 g porcini mushrooms, diced • 100 g porcini mushrooms sliced thinly • 50 g leek chopped finely • 60 g butter • 400 ml vegetable stock • 100 ml cream • 2 g salt • 1 g freshly ground white pepper • 40 g cooked, smoked beef tongue sliced thinly

Method

Cook the leeks and potatoes in vegetable stock for about 30 minutes, till tender, then purée them with a mixer. Use a hot pan to fry the mushrooms in butter, taking care that the juice should not evaporate. When the mushrooms are cooked, add them to the soup which should be brought to the boil again. Finally, stop boiling the soup and purée the mushrooms with the rest. When there are no large pieces in it, add the cream and the rest of the butter (in small pieces) – use a mixer to stir it. Season with salt and pepper.

For serving, add the sliced of smoked beef tongue and thinly sliced raw mushrooms to the soup.

🍷 Recommended wine

Mátraalaji Szürkebarát 2012 – Balázs Ludányi
A complex creamy soup with fresh mushrooms
and smoky flavours. It is very harmonious with
a creamy textured white wine with ripe, fruity
flavours matured in oak barrels.

34 Tokaji Wine Soup

A classic Christmas dish which features on our celebration menu every year. Its speciality is that it is made of our Tokaji wine.

Serves 4

150 ml Tokaji Aszú • 150 ml Tokaji Hársevelű • 4 cloves • 1 allspice • 1 small cinnamon stick • peel of 1 lemon • 8 egg yolks • 20 g sugar

Method

Bring the wine, 400 ml water and the spices to boil in a 1 litre pot with a handle, then simmer it on low heat for about 5 minutes and remove the spices with a small sieve.

Mix the egg yolks and the sugar with a whisk in a mixing bowl until it becomes foamy. Mix it with 100 ml hot, spicy wine and stir it quickly with the whisk, finally pour all the wine in and mix it together.

Prepare the bain-marie (see p. 191), when the water is boiling put the mixing bowl on top, and heat the soup for 3-4 minutes stirring continuously, otherwise egg yolks would shrink.

Serve it hot.

♀ Recommended wine

Tokaji Hárslevelű 2011 – Gróf Degenfeld
The soup reflects the noble, sweet aromas
of Tokaji wines and the matching sweet spices.
A semi sweet Tokaji Hárslevelű, the base
of the soup. is an appropriate choice.

Fillet of Zander, Gundel Style
This dish has always featured on the menu of the
Gundel restaurant, right from the beginning. At first
Europe was not familiar with the technique of
breadcrumbing fish. Gundel recognised the
gastronomic value of this method of preparation and
was among the first restaurateurs to introduce this
novelty originating from Turkey. The popularity of
fresh zander from the Lake Balaton fried golden
brown and served with buttered spinach started to
grow from the beginning of the nineteen hundreds.
This course is a big favourite of many of our guests.

Fish

Catfish with Bacon and Root Vegetables

Paprika Catfish with Bacon Noodles

Catfish 'Tihany' Style

Zander Fish from Lake Balaton 'Rothermere' Style

Filet of Zander 'Gundel' Style

Zander Fish with Porcini Mushrooms
and Dumplings in Butter

Shrimps in Butter Pastry

35 Catfish with Bacon and Root Vegetables

Another classic dish from the 1934 'Dinner Competition'.
The root vegetables can be the best garnish with its colour
and flavours – not to mention how easy it is to prepare.

Serves 4

500 g filet of catfish • 200 g carrots peeled, cut into chunks
• 150 g root parsley peeled, cut into chunks • 100 g kohlrabies
peeled, cut into chunks • 100 g potatoes peeled, cut into chunks
• 50 g celery roots peeled, cut into chunks • 50 g onions peeled,
chopped • 10 g garlic chopped finely, browned in olive oil • 200 g
bacon ground coarsely, fried till crunchy • 2 g fresh thyme • 10 g
parsley chopped finely • juice of 1 lemon, squeezed • 100 ml olive
oil • 150 ml natural yoghurt • 3 g salt • 3 g sugar • 2 g freshly ground
white pepper

Method

Pre-fry the vegetables according to type in a hot pan, then mix and
season with pepper, add thyme and roast in the oven at 160 degrees
Celsius for 20 minutes.

Meanwhile, prepare the catfish: cut into equal size pieces, cover in
olive oil and season with salt and pepper. Fry in a hot pan till both sides
are red, then set aside.

Next, mix the yoghurt with the crunchy garlic, parsley leaves, lemon
juice and a little salt. Before serving, place the fish into the oven at
160 degrees for approx. 3 minutes.

For serving, pour some garlic yoghurt over the fish and sprinkle with
fried bacon.

♟ Recommended wine

Balatonboglári Pirosbor (Siller) 2012
— Géza Légli
Tasteful dish with root vegetables and bacon.
We can look towards the red wines but
choose a light version low on tannins.

36 Paprika Catfish with Bacon Noodles

We really like catfish, because it is easy to obtain fresh all year round. We keep the basic flavours but give new form for this otherwise everyday dish.

Serves 4

600 g catfish filet • 50 g butter • 200 g onion chopped finely • 2 g crushed garlic • 4 g paprika • 2 g freshly ground white pepper • 3 g salt • 2 g hot paprika • 60 g tomatoes (steeped in hot water, peeled, seeds removed), diced 10 x 10 mm • 120 g peppers diced 10 x 10 mm • 400 ml sour cream • 3 eggs • 200 g vermicelli noodles boiled in salty water, then cooled • 100 g bacon chopped finely, fried • 100 ml fish stock (see p. 189)

Method

Use a bowl to mix the noodles with 200 ml sour cream and the whole eggs, then add salt and the fried bacon. Bake in the oven at 95 degrees Celsius for 50 minutes and do not cool before serving. Season the catfish filets with salt and pepper and pre-fry both sides in a pan.

Find a suitable sized pot to brown onions and garlic on medium heat, using melted butter, until golden yellow. Remove the pan from the heat and add paprika, stir, then return to the heat and fry for another minute, stirring continuously. Next, pour 100 ml fish stock into the pan. Return to the heat again and add hot paprika according to taste. Cover and let it simmer on a low heat. After 20 minutes add the tomatoes and freshly diced peppers, then continue simmering for a further 20 minutes. Use a mixer to purée the sauce, and add sour cream for extra richness.

Finally, place the catfish in the hot paprika sauce and bring to the boil. It is now ready to serve.

♈ Recommended wine

Villányi Siller 2012 – Zoltán Gümczer
The colour and taste of paprika determines the choice of wine. This Siller can be a real gastro-wine, which is the perfect partner for the more fatty and spicy fish.

37 Catfish Tihany Style

We consequently pay great attention to have fresh water fishes from Hungary amongst sea water fish as well on our menu, so our guests can choose.

Serves 4

600 g catfish filet • 20 g fresh torn parsley leaves • 20 g fresh parsley chopped finely • 30 g spring onions sliced finely • 30 g leeks • 30 g red onions • 300 g peeled potatoes • 300 g celery roots • 200 g butter • 400 ml milk • 3 g salt • 8 g freshly crushed pepper • 10 ml rapeseed oil • 200 ml demi-glace sauce (see p. 189)

Method

Cook the potatoes and celery separately in boiling salty water. While the vegetables are cooking, cut the catfish filet into 4 equal parts, salt lightly, mix the freshly crushed pepper with chopped parsley and rub the spices gently on one side of the fish (it will stick better if the fish is damp). Pre-fry the fish in a hot pan and set aside.

Begin to brown the onions in rapeseed oil: red onions first, then leeks, and finally the spring onions. Mash the cooked potatoes and celeries, add butter and milk and whisk. Boil the demi-glace dressing, then take it off the heat and let it cool a bit. After a short while, use a mixer to add 150 g cold butter to it.

The last step is roasting the fish: place in the oven at 160 degrees Celsius for about 8 minutes. Prepare a salad using the parsley leaves and a few drops of lukewarm demi-glace dressing, and decorate each piece of fish with it for serving.

Recommended wine

Folly Arborétum Badacsonyörsi Budai Zöld 2011
The vegetables used for cooking this dish provide
stronger flavours. Choose a matching young
white wine with lively tannins and mineral
features from Tihany or around Lake Balaton.

38 Zander Fish from Lake Balaton 'Rothermere' Style

One of Károly Gundel's classic dishes from his 1934 cookbook. It was named after a Hungarian MP of his time.

Serves 4

500 g zander filet without skin • 500 g shrimps • 100 g leeks • 400 g potatoes peeled, diced 10 x 10 mm • 10 g parsley leaves chopped finely • juice of 2 lemons • 300 g butter • 100 ml dry white wine • 8 egg yolks • 3 g salt • 1 g cayenne pepper • 20 g paprika • 500 ml fish stock (see p. 189)

Method

Cook the slices of zander in fish stock. It should take 6 minutes. Make sure that the stock does not boil. When they are cooked, dry the pieces of fish with a dish cloth, place them onto a plate and squeeze lemon juice on them. Prepare hollandaise sauce (thicker than the classical recipe) over steam: start beating the eggs with lemon juice and a little white wine (it is good to boil the wine beforehand). Season with salt, cayenne pepper, and then add some melted butter over the steam, to give the sauce a creamy texture.

Put the potatoes into hot water to boil, and when tender, take $^2/_3$ of them out and set aside. Continue cooking the rest until they are overdone. Melt butter in a pan and start browning the boiled potatoes that were taken out earlier, seasoning with salt. When they start to brown, add the parsley and continue frying. Finally, add the overcooked potatoes and stir. The result is a cross between mashed potatoes and boiled potatoes with parsley.

Fry the fish, coat in thick hollandaise sauce and then place into the oven at 180 degrees Celsius for 3 minutes.

Make shrimp ragout: steam the leeks in butter and when tender, add the shrimps and the remaining parsley. Add a few drops of white wine, sprinkle paprika on top and finish cooking immediately. It is now ready to serve.

♆ Recommended wine

Csopaki Olaszrizling 2011
– Mihály Figula / Gundel Selection
The marriage of a creamy, buttery sauce, the
zander fish and the shrimp stew requires a full
bodied white wine from Lake Balaton with rich
flavours. An intensive Italian Riesling rich in mineral
taste, matured in wooden barrels can provide an
excellent harmony.

39 Fillet of Zander 'Gundel' Style

One of our most popular dishes which is featured on all menus. The ingredients are from the old recipe but we changed the preparation method according to more modern times.

Serves 4

560 g boneless zander, cut into 4 slices • 3 g salt • 200 ml fish stock (see p. 189) made from the zander bones • 50 ml dry white wine • 200 ml cream • 2 egg yolks • 300 ml béchamel sauce • 200 g mushrooms fried, chopped finely • 600 g fresh spinach, tough stems removed, washed • 100 g butter • 40 g breadcrumbs • 1 g freshly ground white pepper • 20 g corn flour • 20 g chopped fresh parsley leaves • 10 g fresh parsley leaves • 10 g dill • 10 g chives, chopped • Vegetable pearls: 2 potatoes, peeled • 2 carrots, peeled • 2 zucchinis • salt

Method

For the vegetable pearls using a small melon scoop, hollow pearls from the potatoes, carrots and zucchini. Bring 2 small saucepans of water to a boil over high heat. Add the potatoes to one and the carrots to the other and cook for about 10 minutes until tender. A few minutes before the vegetables are done, bring a third saucepan of water to a boil and cook the zucchini for about 1 minute until tender. Drain all 3 vegetables and mix together in one strainer. Melt the butter in a small frying pan. Add the vegetables and toss to coat. Add the parsley, season to taste with salt and cook over medium heat for about 3 minutes, tossing, until heated through. Cover and keep warm.

Bechamel sauce (see p. 186): In a saucepan, combine the fish stock and wine, bring to a boil over medium heat and cook until reduced by about a third. In a separate saucepan, bring the cream to a boil over medium-high heat and cook until reduced by half. Slowly pour the stock into the cream, stirring to mix. Season to taste with salt, bring to a boil and cook for about 5 minutes until slightly thickened. Cover to keep warm.

Sprinkle the fish fillets lightly with salt and roll in flour. Heat the oil in a large, deep frying pan. Fry the fish for 6 or 7 minutes, turning one, until opaque and cooked through. Serve immediately.

♀ Recommended wine

Figula Mihály Balatonszőlősi Sauvignon Blanc
2011 – Gundel Selection
Speciality made with different vegetables,
spinach and bechamel sauce. Choose a wine
with fresh, green fruity flavours, crispy tannins
which is more mature.

40 Zander Fish with Porcini Mushrooms and Dumplings in Butter

This dish was also amongst the winners of the 1934 'Dinner Competition'. The garnish was invented in the modern era, but otherwise the original recipe remained unchanged.

Serves 4

500 g zander, skin on • 150 g porcini mushrooms, diced 10 x 10 mm • 50 g porcini mushrooms chopped finely • 100 g onions • 100 ml vegetable broth (see p. 191) • 1 egg yolk • 1 egg white • 200 g butter • 100 ml whipped cream • 90 g flour • 10 g parsley leaves chopped finely • 10 g paprika • 5 g salt • 2 g freshly ground • pepper • For the dumplings: 3 egg yolks • 3 egg whites, beaten hard • 60 g butter at room temperature • 270 g white flour

Method

First, fry the finely chopped onions in butter, then add a small amount of vegetable stock, bring to the boil and let it evaporate. Repeat at least 3 times. When the onions are tender, season with paprika – this will be your sauce base. Purée with a mixer and set aside.

Next, sprinkle salt and pepper on the fish, then pre-cook it in a pan. Meanwhile, boil salt water for the dumplings. To finish the sauce off, bring it to the boil and add the larger pieces of mushroom to it. Stir, then add whipped cream and mix the butter in gently, making the sauce creamy and glistening. Before serving, when the sauce is still warm but not piping hot, add the raw, finely chopped porcini mushrooms. Meanwhile, preheat the oven to 180 degrees and place the fish inside for 4 minutes.

Prepare the dumplings with butter (see p. 189). Before serving, add a little butter and parsley.

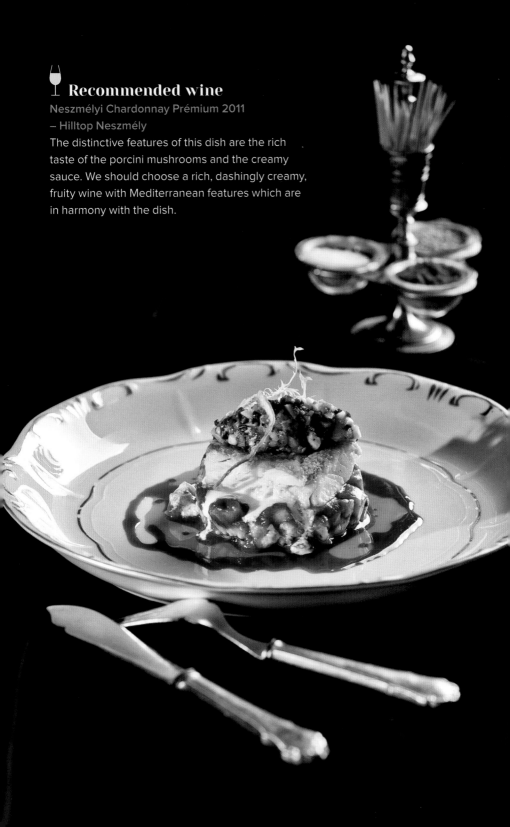

♾ Recommended wine

Neszmélyi Chardonnay Prémium 2011
– Hilltop Neszmély

The distinctive features of this dish are the rich taste of the porcini mushrooms and the creamy sauce. We should choose a rich, dashingly creamy, fruity wine with Mediterranean features which are in harmony with the dish.

41 Shrimps in Butter Pastry

A classic winter dish of our own. It is not too difficult to prepare but the result is very attractive and delicious.

Serves 4

250 g shrimps minced finely • 250 g bread rolls soaked into cream, ground • 20 g fresh coriander chopped finely • 20 g fresh parsley leaves chopped finely • 10 g fresh chives • 2 hard-boiled eggs chopped finely • 10 g paprika • 500 g butter pastry • 1 egg • 150 g rocket salad • 100 ml mayonnaise • 100 ml sour cream • juice of 1 lime squeezed • 2 g freshly ground white pepper • 3 g salt

Method

For the filling, mix the shrimps with soaked bread rolls, parsley, coriander, paprika, freshly ground white pepper and season lightly with salt.

Prepare the pastry: on a floury surface, roll it to become 2 mm thin. Distribute the filling evenly over the pastry and roll it up like a strudel. Cool well before baking. Preheat the oven to 190 degrees Celsius and bake the pastry for approx. 12 minutes. While it is baking, prepare the rocket salad for serving by letting it soak for 3 minutes.

Mix the mayonnaise with sour cream in a bowl, add the fresh pepper, the lime juice and chives.

🍷 **Recommended wine**

Csopaki Olaszrizling 2011
– Mihály Figula / Gundel Selection
This dish has the special, unique flavours of the shrimps. The right choice is a sophisticated, elegant, complex, full bodied white wine.

Poultry

Paprika Chicken

Duck Leg with Cherries, Kohlrabi Purée
and Stewed Radish

Slow Roast Duck Breast

Dove Breast with Puréed Vegetables
and Leeks in Cream

Pan Fried Foie Gras in Apple Sauce
and Egg Barley with Cabbage

42 Paprika Chicken

It is an iconic Hungarian dish. There is everything in it that people associate with Hungarian cuisine: paprika, tomato and onions.

Serves 4

2 whole chickens, quartered and trimmed • 100 duck fat • 200 ml chicken stock (see p. 190) • 200 g onions, finely chopped • 2 g garlic, crushed • 20 g sweet Hungarian paprika • 3 g salt • hot Hungarian paprika to taste • 60 g tomato, peeled, seeded and cubed (10 x 10 mm) • 120 g green bell peppers, seeded and diced (10 x 10 mm) • 200 ml sour cream • 100 g butter • egg dumplings (see p. 189)

Method

In a large pot, heat the duck fat over medium heat. Add the onions and sauté until golden brown. Remove from heat, add the garlic and the sweet paprika and stir well. Start heating the pot again, stirring continuously. After 1 minute, add 100 ml chicken stock.

Add the chicken legs, salt and hot paprika to taste. Cover and cook over low heat for 20 minutes. Add the breasts and the tomatoes and simmer for about 20 minutes longer or until the chicken is cooked through and tender. Lift the chicken from the pot and set aside.

Add the green peppers to the pot and simmer for about 15 minutes in the sauce.

Purée the sauce and add sour cream.

When the chicken is cool enough to handle, remove the skin and cut the meat from the bones, keeping the breasts and thighs intact. Add the bones to the sauce and bring to a boil.

Fry the dumplings in butter before serving.

♀ Recommended wine

Szekszárdi Kékfrankos Rozé 2012 – Tamás Dúzsi
The dish plays a leading part in traditional
Hungarian cuisine. It is more spicy with paprika
flavours and colours, so one of the popular, real,
fresh rosés is a good choice.

43 Duck Leg with Cherries, Kohlrabi Purée and Stewed Radish

One of the most authentic dishes of our restaurant, in which every one can appreciate the simple, delicious food and dining.

Serves 4

500 g cherries • 500 g fresh kohlrabies • 500 g radish with leaves • 500 g potatoes • 5 g salt • 2 g freshly ground white pepper • 4 duck legs • 1 kg duck fat • 150 g butter • 200 g onions • 50 g sugar • 100 ml red wine

Method

24 hours before cooking, marine the duck legs with salt (only on the side with the skin on). The next day heat up the duck fat, put the legs in and cook it slowly on 90 degrees (duck confit, see p. 191). The fat should not boil. It is ready when the bones can be wound out of the duck legs. Before serving grill the legs in the oven on 190 degrees until they are red.

During confit, peel all the vegetables.

Start boiling the kohlrabies, potatoes with half of the onions. When they are soft pour out the water and purée them. Put half of the butter in it before serving. Cut the radishes into half and stew them in butter.

For the cherry ragout, remove the stones from the cherries, melt sugar in a pan until it is slightly caramellized. Pour the cherries into it. After sautéing for a minute, start adding the red wine and pour it all in. Reduce it (see p. 190), then remove it from the heat, wait, and when it is cool mix it with 50 g butter.

Prepare only as much as we can eat, and serve it at room temperature.

♀ Recommended wine

Egri Pinot Noir 2009 – Nimród Kovács

The ripe, red fruits and the brown-coloured duck
meet in this dish. It requires the queen of red wines,
which features strong cherry flavours.

44 Slow Roast Duck Breast

One of our most loved spring dish which features on our menu all year round.

Serves 4

800 g young duck's breast with the skin on • 600 g potatoes, peeled • 100 g onions, chopped • 50 g chopped parsley • 400 g pitted cherries • 200 ml full-bodied red wine • 120 g butter • 2 g salt • 6 g sugar • 1 g freshly ground white pepper

Method

Prepare the duck breasts 12 hours prior to cooking. Separate the meat from the thick layers of fat, and marinate both meat and fat in brining (see p. 187) for 6 hours. After this, place the meat into a cool, dry place in the fridge.

Mince the thick layer of duck fat and start frying to extract the gravy. You will need both the gravy and the crispy skin later. Pre-cook the duck breasts in their own gravy, seasoned with pepper. When both sides of the meat are reddened, place in the oven for 60 minutes at 68 degrees Celsius.

Meanwhile, boil the potatoes until soft. Strain to remove excess water. Fry the onions in hot duck fat, then add the potatoes in and fry them with the onions.

Melt sugar in another frying pan. When it is brown, pour the red wine over it slowly. When all the wine is gone, boil for another minute before adding the pitted cherries. Simmer for one minute, then remove from the heat and let it cool. When it is starting to cool down, stir the cold butter in until the sauce is creamy and glistening. Let the duck rest, reheat the potatoes and mix the parsley in. The sauce does not need to be hot for serving.

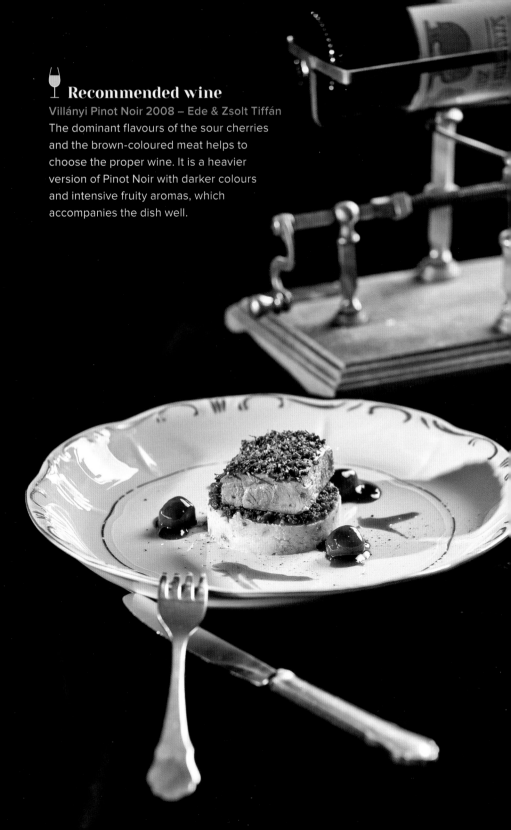

♟ Recommended wine
Villányi Pinot Noir 2008 – Ede & Zsolt Tiffán
The dominant flavours of the sour cherries
and the brown-coloured meat helps to
choose the proper wine. It is a heavier
version of Pinot Noir with darker colours
and intensive fruity aromas, which
accompanies the dish well.

45 Dove Breast with Puréed Vegetables and Leeks in Cream

People used to eat dove in the countryside. These days it has to feature in all good restaurants' menu because it is very unique.

Serves 4

4 dove breasts on the bone, skin on • 3 g salt • 3 g sugar • 5 fresh stalks of thyme • 1 g freshly ground white pepper • 200 g butter • 100 g olive oil• 180 ml cream• 200 g celery roots peeled, sliced • 200 g carrots peeled, sliced• 300 g peas • 100 g potatoes peeled, sliced • 50 g parsley leaves chopped finely • 200 g leeks chopped into 2 cm pieces

Method

Prepare the dove breasts at room temperature (never cook meat straight out of the fridge, always start grilling from room temperature). Start boiling the vegetables in water seasoned with sugar and salt, using just enough water to cover them. Celeries and carrots do not contain starch, so we need to add potatoes – it is impossible to prepare a nice purée without them. However, the flavour of the potatoes should not be dominant, therefore do not use make the potatoes more than 1/3 of the vegetables (eg. 50 g potatoes for 200 g celeries). Do not boil the peas, just pour boiling water over them, then swap the water for cream. Purée the vegetables. Cook till tender, and set aside for serving.

Fry the dove breasts in a hot pan with olive oil and pepper (but no salt). When the pre-cooking is finished, carefully remove the meat from the bones (you will need the pan later). Place into the oven at 85 degrees Celsius for approx. 10 minutes with a stick of thyme.

Finish the purée off: while simmering slowly, add cold butter, and stir until smooth. When everything is ready to serve, put the pan back on the heat and fry the dove breasts until crispy. Use another pan to brown the leeks for 2 minutes, then add cream, pepper, salt and chopped parsley leaves.

♟ Recommended wine

Egri Leányka 2009 – Tamás Pók

The creamy leeks and the more sweet vegetable purée determine the choice of wine which is mature and complete, it has grassy flavours and subtle tannins.

46 Pan Fried Foie Gras in Apple Sauce and Egg Barley with Cabbage

Foie gras plays an important part in our restaurant's life.
We aim to have it on the menu in different varieties. Cabbage and egg barley is the more sophisticated version of cabbage pasta.

Serves 4

640 g goose liver • 4 red apples, peeled, cubed into 10 x 10 mm pieces • 400 g white cabbage, grated • 20 g garlic, chopped finely • 100 g egg barley • 100 g duck fat • 3 g salt • 1 g freshly ground white pepper • 4 g sugar • 50 g potatoes peeled, grated • 100 ml dry white wine

Method

Brown the cabbage on a little duck fat, adding salt, pepper and the potatoes. Make sure they are not overdone, 10 minutes should be sufficient. In the meantime, boil the egg barley in lightly salted water. Strain and set aside when ready.

Use a pan to caramelise the sugar; when it is golden yellow, pour the wine into it gradually, and stir until it thickens. Add the apples and then remove from the heat immediately. Fry the egg barley with the cabbage and season.

Cut the goose liver into equal sized strips. Season with pepper and start frying in a hot pan. While frying, moisten the goose liver with its own fat. It will be done in approx. 4-6 minutes.

Let it rest for 2 more minutes, and then it is ready to serve. Since salt does not dissolve in fat, lightly sprinkle the livers with salt after cooking.

♍ Recommended wine

Somlói Juhfark 2009 – Tornai Cellar
The apple stew, the egg barley with cabbage and
the dry white wine used in making the dish require
a non-sweet wine. We recommend a full bodied
Somlói with intensive white fruity flavours,
matured in wooden barrels.

Veal Chops 'Pittsburgh' Style

In 1939 the mayor of Budapest invited the mayor of Pittsburgh, USA to a visit to the capital city. This dish was prepared and served by Károly Gundel at the banquette organised in his honour. It was then added to the permanent menu of the Gundel House and was also offered at the World Fair in New York, when the New York Times wrote that the Gundel restaurant did more to enhance Hungary's reputation than a shipload of tourist brochures could have done.

Meat dishes

Fresh Kohlrabi Stuffed with Veal

Goulash for Lords with Dumplings Royale

Veal Chops 'Pittsburgh' Style

Tenderloin 'Gundel' Style

Gundel Ragout 'Tokány' Style

Boiled Lamb Trotters with Creamy Polenta

47 Fresh Kohlrabi Stuffed with Veal

A perfect spring dish, one of the favourites of our guests. One of our determining seasonal daily offers.

Serves 4

10 whole kohlrabies (fresh, with leaves) • 300 g minced veal (not too dry) • 300 g white bread or rolls soaked in milk • 200 ml sour cream • 200 g butter • 10 g fresh sage • 50 g fresh parsley leaves without stalks • 100 g potatoes peeled, sliced thinly • 50 g spring onions sliced thinly • 3 g salt • 2 g sugar • 1 g hot paprika, ground

Method

Remove the kohlrabi leaves. Do not throw them away, but soak in water and when crunchy, cut into thin strips. Cut the tops of the kohlrabies off (they do not need to peeled) and then carve the centre of the kohlrabies out with a spoon, removing most of the inside and leaving only the outer layer.

Boil water with sugar and salt to approx. 90 degrees Celsius. When the water is warm, boil the cut-off kohlrabi tops in it for 5 minutes, then cool immediately to preserve the colour.

Next, boil the carved out kohlrabi shells too, this should take approx. 10 minutes. In the meantime, start cooking the ingredients for the sauce in a smaller pot: the potatoes and the insides of the kohlrabies. Use the same stock (with salt and sugar), approx. 200 ml.

For the stuffing, mix the minced veal and the soaked bread in a bowl. Season with salt, pepper, sage and leek; mix well. Stuff the carved out kohlrabies with it until full. When all the ingredients of the sauce are soft, use a mixer to purée the sauce.

Place all the stuffed kohlrabies into a large pot with a lid, and pour the sauce underneath them. Simmer on low heat for approx. 30 minutes. To complete the sauce, gradually add sour cream and butter while simmering. Sprinkle with spring onions and strips of kohlrabi leaves. Serve immediately.

🍷 Recommended wine

János Hegyi Sauvignon Blanc 2012 – Ottó Légli
Butter-soft veal flavoured with the original tastes
of the kohlrabi. We can try a full bodied white
wine rich in vegetable aromas, matured in
wooden barrels.

48 Goulash for Lords with Dumplings Royale

Traditional steak dish with unusual choice of garnish.
The real Hungarian flavours always featured on our menu, showing that traditions play an important part in our restaurant's life.

Serves 4

500 g joints of beef • 100 g celery roots • 150 g dumplings, cooked (see p. 189) • 100 g onions chopped finely • 100 g ripe tomatoes peeled and cubed • 100 g green peppers • 100 g leeks chopped finely • 200 ml beef stock • 100 ml cream • 3 eggs • 20 g garlic sliced thinly • 20 g paprika • 100 g duck fat • 3 g salt • 1 g freshly ground white pepper • 1 g cumin seeds, crushed in a mortar

Method

First, fry the onions in duck fat. Season with crushed garlic and finely chopped celery. Next, add the beef stock gradually and simmer for 2 hours, until the broth thickens. Sprinkle the paprika into it towards the end. While the sauce is cooking, we can start roasting the meat.

Season the joints of beef on both sides and pre-cook them in a hot frying pan. Then roast in the oven at 82 degrees Celsius till they are medium (this should take approx. 2 hours).

While the sauce and meat are cooking we can prepare the dumplings royale. We will need the dumplings, the cream and the whole eggs. Mix the eggs with the cream, season with salt and pour over the dumplings. Place them into a deep, oven-proof dish and bake in the oven, alongside the meat, at 82 degrees Celsius for approx 45 minutes.

When the beef is ready, raise the temperature of the oven and roast for a further 5 minutes. Before serving, glaze the green pepper, leek and peeled tomatoes in a hot pan. Be careful not to overcook them.

♟ Recommended wine

Villányi Grand Reserve 2006
– Vylyan / Gundel Selection
A classic dish made of beef loin with
significant flavours and roasted vegetables.
Full bodied 'gentlemanly' red wines rich in
tannins are a good choice for this dish.

49 Veal Chops 'Pittsburgh' Style

Modern version of a traditional Gundel recipe which has featured on the menu for about 60 years.

Serves 4

700 g veal chops • 160 g goose liver, cut into 4 slices • 200 g champignon mushrooms, chopped • 10 ml truffle oil • 10 g chopped parsley • 40 g bacon, cut into strips, fried till crunchy 150 g brown sauce (see p. 187) • 400 g hominy • 100 ml dry red wine, reduced • 100 g butter • 3 g salt • 1 g cayenne pepper

Method

Fry the onions in bacon fat, then add the strips of crunchy bacon. Add 150 ml brown sauce and boil for 1 minute. Add the red wine (reduced to half the original quantity) and boil for a further minute, then set the sauce aside until serving.

In a large frying pan, heat oil over high heat. Add the chops, cut into 170 g pieces, season with pepper and sauté until browned on both sides. Transfer to a roasting pan and roast in a preheated oven at 85 degrees Celsius for about 15 minutes, until medium rare.

While the meet is cooking, prepare the hominy (see p. 190). Cut into 4 pieces, fry in oil and then place in the oven to roast with the veal.

In a frying pan, heat oil and sauté the goose livers for 2 minutes on each side. Season with salt and pepper. Drain on paper towels, patting the liver slices to remove as much oil as possible.

Before serving, bring the sauce to the boil and add cold butter for creaminess. A few drops of truffle oil will give it a unique flavour.

♟ Recommended wine

Szekszárdi Bikavér 2008 Ferenc Takler
– Gundel Selection

Interesting mixture of flavours predominate this
dish with veal, goose liver, an aromatic sauce
and the creamy corn. Our choice is one of our
successful medium bodied, complex red wines
from Takler Cellar with mature tannins.

50 Tenderloin 'Gundel' Style

Tenderloin is one of the most emblematic parts of the beef.
To prepare it well, one needs lot of experience and knowledge.

Serves 4

560 g tenderloin • 150 g porcini mushrooms sliced, fried • 300 g spinach • 50 g chives chopped finely • 100 g bacon fried, crunchy • 150 g fresh white breadcrumbs • 1 egg • 2 egg yolks • 200 g butter • 300 ml supreme sauce (see p. 190) • 300 g mashed potatoes • 200 g cleaned butter (see p. 189)

Method

First, clean the tenderloin, salt it, and coat the meat in eggs and breadcrumbs (do not use flour). Use a pan to fry them on both sides in a little bit of cleaned butter.

Next, fry the spinach quickly in butter, strain it to get rid of any excess liquid, then chop finely and set aside.

Place the pieces of meat on a baking tray and cover evenly in fried spinach, then sprinkle sliced mushrooms (previously fried in butter) on top.

Add egg yolks to the mashed potatoes and spread the mixture on top of the mushrooms. Sprinkle some breadcrumbs on top and cook in the oven at 180 degrees Celsius for 3 minutes. Serve with crunchy fried bacon, and supreme sauce, mixed with chives.

🍷 **Recommended wine**

Villányi Cabernet Franc 2008
– Matias Cellar / Gundel Selection

Our speciality with noble red meat, forest
mushroom flavours and creamy texture. Its
perfect pair is the perfectly matured, spicy
Cabernet Franc in Barrique barrels from
Matias Cellar in Villány.

51 Gundel Ragout 'Tokány' Style

The son of Károly Gundel, Imre wrote the following about this dish: 'Please, dear Reader, the list of ingredients of this cavalcade of flavours are beef tenderloin and goose liver, asparagus, mushrooms, green beans and red wine. There is nothing else in it... but you do not need any more either, I think!'

Serves 4

150 g butter • 50 ml cream • 1 egg • 100 g leek, chopped • 250 g button mushrooms, sliced • 100 g chopped fresh parsley leaves • 400 ml brown sauce (see p. 187) • 200 ml full bodied red wine, such as Gundel Egri Merlot • 150 g white asparagus, cut into 30 mm lengths • 100 g green beans, cut into 30 mm lengths • 720 g beef tenderloin, about 8 mm thick, trimmed and cut into 40 mm strips • 200 g goose liver, cut into 4 slices • 3 g salt • 1 g freshly ground white pepper • 500 g dumplings (see p. 189)

Method

Sauce: in a frying pan, melt the butter. Add the leeks and sauté until transparent. Cook for about 3 minutes or longer until tender. Add the mushrooms and sauté for 3 minutes longer. Season with parsley leaves, salt and pepper. In a saucepan, bring the red wine to a boil and cook for 10 to 15 minutes until reduced to 2 tablespoons. Add the leeks and mushroom mixture. Add the brown sauce, stir and simmer for 5 minutes. Cover and set aside to keep warm.

Vegetables: cook the asparagus and the green beans separately in lightly salted water for about 10 minutes each. Cover and set aside. Reheat in the cooking water just before serving.

Meat: sprinkle the goose liver lightly with salt. In a small frying pan, heat 1 tablespoon of oil and fry for 2 minutes on each side. Remove from the pan, cover and set aside to keep warm.

In a separate frying pan, heat the remaining oil over high heat. Add the tenderloin strips, season with salt and pepper, and sauté for about 6 minutes, turning the meat several times, until cooked. (You may have to use 2 pans or cook the meat in batches. Do not crowd the pan.)

Stir the meat into the hot mushroom sauce.

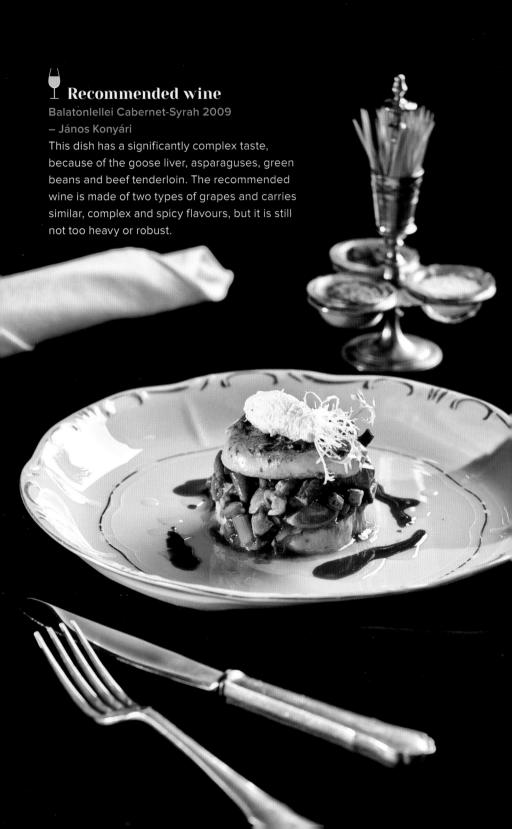

Recommended wine

Balatonlellei Cabernet-Syrah 2009
– János Konyári

This dish has a significantly complex taste, because of the goose liver, asparaguses, green beans and beef tenderloin. The recommended wine is made of two types of grapes and carries similar, complex and spicy flavours, but it is still not too heavy or robust.

52 Boiled Lamb Trotters with Creamy Polenta

A more complex dish which takes a day to prepare.

Serves 4

4 lamb trotters (front legs) • 200 g peeled carrots, diced • 200 g peeled root parsley, diced • 200 g peeled kohlrabies, diced • 200 g peeled onions, diced • 200 g peeled tomatoes, diced • 200 g celery stalks, diced • 200 g leeks, diced • 50 g fresh parsley, chopped finely • 20 g garlic chopped finely • 30 g capers • 1 rosemary • 10 g flour • 200 g butter • 100 ml olive oil • 100 g cream cheese • 400 ml milk • 200 g corn flour • 4 g salt • 20 g sugar • 500 ml red wine • 500 ml meat stock (see p. 190)

Method

You will need 1 day to prepare this dish.

Soak the lamb trotters in brining (see p. 187) for 6 hours, then fry them in olive oil using a hot pan. Prepare the sauce: brown the sugar, then add the carrots, root parsley, kohlrabi, onions, garlic and continue frying them. Add red wine and let it evaporate. Make beurre manié (see p. 186) which will gradually thicken the sauce. Cook the sauce for approx. 3 hours. When it is ready, place the lamb trotters into a deep dish and splash with sauce generously. Cover and roast in the oven at 85 degrees Celsius for at least 5 hours (or until the meat comes off the bone).

Let's make the hominy (see p. 190).

Before serving, finish the sauce by removing any excess grease from the top, and purée it with a mixer. When it is nice and smooth, add cold butter to it gradually. Heat olive oil in a pan and fry the celery stalk, tomatoes and leek. Throw in the capers and stir. Before serving the polenta, add cream cheese and cold butter for extra creaminess.

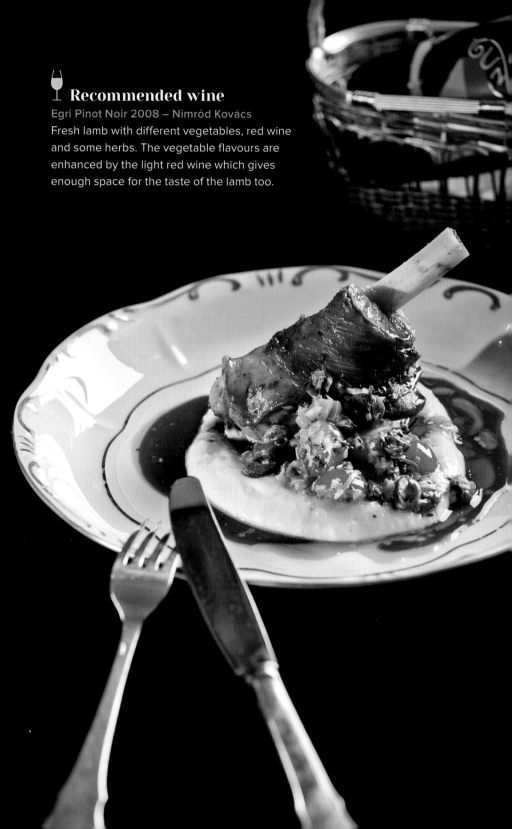

Recommended wine

Egri Pinot Noir 2008 – Nimród Kovács
Fresh lamb with different vegetables, red wine and some herbs. The vegetable flavours are enhanced by the light red wine which gives enough space for the taste of the lamb too.

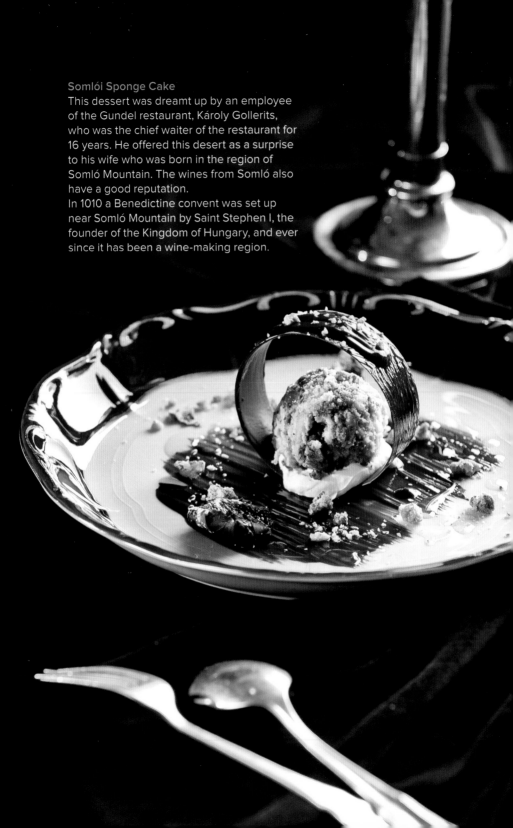

Somlói Sponge Cake

This dessert was dreamt up by an employee
of the Gundel restaurant, Károly Gollerits,
who was the chief waiter of the restaurant for
16 years. He offered this desert as a surprise
to his wife who was born in the region of
Somló Mountain. The wines from Somló also
have a good reputation.

In 1010 a Benedictine convent was set up
near Somló Mountain by Saint Stephen I, the
founder of the Kingdom of Hungary, and ever
since it has been a wine-making region.

Desserts

Cabbage Pancakes with Caramel Sauce

Hungarian Cottage Cheese Dumplings 'Wampetics' Style

Gundel's Sweet Cottage Cheese Pastry

Bread Pudding with Apricot Jam

Strudel Variations

Hungarian Style Layered Walnut Pastry

Gundel Crêpe

Baked Prune Pancakes

Somlói Sponge Cake

Gundel Chocolate Mousse

Gundel Parfait

Chocolate Parfait with Goat Cheese

Strawberries with Meringue and Tokaji Wine

Chocolate and Raspberry Cake

Chocolate Napoleon

Chocolate Lava (Soufflé)

Gundel Chocolate and Marzipan Cake

Chocolate and Nut Slice

53 Cabbage Pancakes with Caramel Sauce

One of the classic recipes of the original Gundel cook book. Many people like cabbage pasta sweet. In here, the cabbage is stuffed into pancakes.

Serves 4

200 g white cabbage, grated finely • 1 egg • 1 egg yolk • 100 ml milk • 100 ml water • 60 g sugar • 80 g white flour • 4 g salt • 1 g freshly ground black pepper • 20 g cleaned butter (see p. 189) **• 30 g butter • 20 ml cream**

Method

Cover the cabbage generously in salt. Let it stand for one hour, then squeeze the juice out of it. In a hot frying pan, brown half of the sugar on cleaned butter. Add the cabbage, season with pepper and sauté until soft.

Prepare the pancake mix in the meantime: mix the milk with water, a whole egg and an egg yolk, 10 g sugar and 1 g salt, then add flour and stir until the mixture is smooth. When the cabbage is soft, squeeze it out again, keeping the juice for later. Add the squeezed cabbage leaves to the pancake mix and set aside to rest.

For the caramel sauce, brown sugar in a pan. When it is golden brown, dilute it with the cabbage juice. Boil and reduce to a third of the original quantity, then stop boiling and add the cream in. Put cold butter in too, for increased creaminess.

Fry the pancakes on butter in a hot pan. Serve hot.

Recommended wine

Móri Ezerjó 2006 – István Bozóky
Interesting dessert accompanied with caramel
sauce. It requires a sweet dessert wine with lively
tannins, high enough sugar contents and significant
aromas of honey and spices.

54 Hungarian Cottage Cheese Dumplings 'Wampetics' Style

The dish was named after the owner of the restaurant which used to stand on the same spot before Gundel opened.
The uniqueness of the dish comes from the strawberries which can be stuffed into the dumplings, or just decorate the plates.

Serves 6

500 g cottage cheese or quark · 10 g butter · 150 ml sour cream · 6 g semolina · 2.5 g flour · 2 eggs · 1 egg yolk · 7.5 g breadcrumbs · 30 g sugar · 20 g icing sugar

Method

First, use a sieve to break the cottage cheese, then mix it with the eggs, semolina, 5 g butter, the sugar and a pinch of salt. Form dumplings approx. 6 cm in diameter using this mixture. Boil them in salty hot water. Serve the dumplings coated in breadcrumbs, previously toasted on hot butter and the icing sugar.

Put a spoonful or two of sour cream on top to finish.

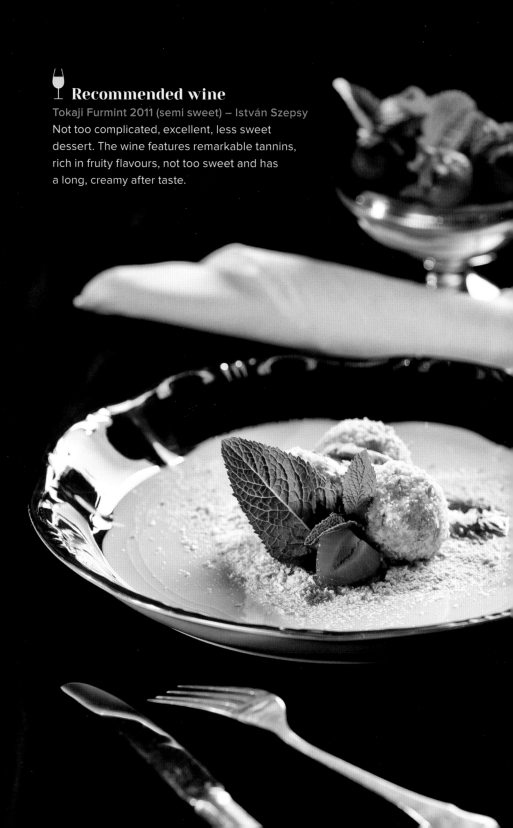

♟ Recommended wine

Tokaji Furmint 2011 (semi sweet) – István Szepsy
Not too complicated, excellent, less sweet
dessert. The wine features remarkable tannins,
rich in fruity flavours, not too sweet and has
a long, creamy after taste.

55 Gundel's Sweet Cottage Cheese Pastry

A classic one amongst the Gundel desserts. Its uniqueness comes from the locally made apricot jam.

Serves 4

350 g flour • 130 g butter • 150 g icing sugar, plus a little extra for sprinkling • 2 egg yolks • a pinch of salt • 100 g apricot jam • 500 g cottage cheese or quark • 150 g caster sugar • 5 eggs • 500 ml sour cream • the juice and grated peel of 1 lemon

Method

First, knead all the ingredients (apart from the jam) to make an even dough mix, then let it rest in the fridge for an hour. After an hour, use half of the dough to line a baking tray and spread home-made chunky apricot jam onto the layer of uncooked dough.

Use a fork to break the cottage cheese or quark, then mix it with the egg yolks, sour cream, half of the sugar, lemon juice and grated lemon peel. Meanwhile, beat the egg whites with the remaining sugar and gently stir them into the cottage cheese. Spread the resulting mixture onto the prepared pastry on the baking tray, then use the remaining dough to form strips – they should be the width of a little finger. Lay the strips on top of the filling, forming a grid. (Alternatively, grate the pastry on a large-holed grater and sprinkle the bits on top of the filling). Bake in the oven at 160 degrees for approx. 30 minutes until golden brown.

Before serving, put a little apricot jam on top of the pastry and sprinkle with icing sugar.

♟ Recommended wine

Tokaji Áts Cuvée 2011 (sweet) – Royal Tokaj
Light desert with citrus and apricot flavours.
The wine is a mariage of overripe grapes which
features the same aromas as the dessert.

56 Bread Pudding with Apricot Jam

One of the chef's favourite desserts. An everyday dessert which can be served, according to taste, with vanilla or chocolate sauce as well, instead of the jam.

Serves 6

700 g milk-loaf • 5 eggs • 5 egg yolks • 700 ml milk • 30 g sugar • 10 g icing sugar • the inside of 1 vanilla stick, carved out • 20 g butter • 40 g apricot jam • 10 ml rum

Method

First, cut the milk-loaf into 15 mm thick slices. Toast on both sides and spread with butter while still hot, letting the butter melt. Mix all the milk with the vanilla, sugar and eggs, as well as the 5 egg yolks. Layer the slices of bread in a deep, heatproof dish. Splash the sugary milk and eggs generously on each layer. When all the bread is in the dish, pour the remaining milk over it and let it stand for an hour before baking.

Meanwhile, start preparing the sauce: heat the jam, add the vanilla seeds and rum and bring to the boil slowly. When it has boiled, set aside till serving.

Preheat the oven to 95 degrees Celsius and bake the pudding for 50 minutes. After 50 minutes, take it out of the oven and sprinkle icing sugar on top. Turn the heat up to 180 degrees and bake for a further 5 minutes. Slice when warm, and serve with hot apricot jam.

♆ Recommended wine

Mátraaljai Sárgamuskotály 2009 (sweet)
– Attila Gábor Németh

This dessert is easy to make, its main ingredient
is the tasty apricot jam. The wine is the work
of artisians. The overripe Muscat grapes
perfumed, fruity aromas and surprisingly
nice tannins meet in harmony.

57 Strudel Variations

Strudels so belong to Gundel's image that no day can start without them.

Serves 4

Strudel pastry: vegetable strudel (see p. 64) • Apple strudel:
1.5 kg apples • 1 g ground cinnamon • 100 g icing sugar • peel
and juice of 1 lemon • 30 g butter • 100 g breadcrumbs • Sour
cherry strudel: sour cherry • Cottage cheese strudel: 500 g
cottage cheese or quark • 150 g caster sugar • 30 g semolina
• 10 g raisins • 3 eggs • peel and juice of 1 lemon

Method

First, peel the apples and cut the core out, then dice and sprinkle a little cinnamon with sugar on them. Next, add lemon juice and lemon peel for flavour and steam briefly (if there is too much apple juice, add ground walnuts to absorb it). Sprinkle lukewarm butter onto the rolled pastry, then dust with breadcrumbs, and cover half of the pastry with apple filling. Roll up to make strudel.

Sour cherry strudel : pit the sour cherries and make the filling identically to the apple strudel.

Cottage cheese strudel: put the cottage cheese through a sieve and then flavour with half of the sugar plus the lemon juice and lemon peel. Mix the egg yolks into it. Beat the egg whites with the remaining half of the sugar and then mix them with the cottage cheese. Soak the raisins in water, and add them to the mixture. Use a spoon to place the filling onto the side of the strudel pastry, then roll it up.

♀ Recommended wine

Tokaji Aszú 5 Puttonyos 2003
– Gundel Selection

Multi-flavoured, traditional dessert selection.
The complexity, sweetness, fruitiness and
tannins of the wine predominate superbly
with desserts like this.

58 Hungarian Style Layered Walnut Pastry

A recipe from the original 1939 cookbook. A perfect companion to quick lunches or dinners – ideal with 'Palóc' soup or a Goulash.

Serves 12

4 packs of puff pastry • 500 g walnuts • 500 g icing sugar • 150 g raisins • 40 g butter • 50 ml rum • 100 ml cream • grated peel of 1 lemon • 1 g ground cinnamon • 1 g nutmeg

Method

Mix the ground walnuts with icing sugar. Add the raisins (washed, soaked in rum) and mix the nutmeg, lemon peel and cinnamon in for extra flavour.

Pour cream over the mixture and heat it all together until the sugar melts. Spread 2-3 layers of butter on the puff pastry and place on a buttered baking tray. Spread some of the filling on the pastry, then add another layer of pastry and another layer of filling. Continue this way up to 10 layers.

Bake on a slow heat (at 140 degrees Celsius) and serve hot.

Cut into squares, sprinkling icing sugar on top.

Recommended wine

Tokaji Aszú 2007 – Royal Tokaj
Intensively sweet, rum, raisin and citrus flavoured
spicy dish. The wine is a bit more significant
because of its sweetness, citrus-fruity flavours
and excellent tannins.

59 Gundel Crêpe

Undoubtedly the most iconic dish of our restaurant. It is really popular and every year we make more than 10 thousand of them.

10 servings

2 large eggs • 240 g flour • 300 ml milk • 300 g seltzer water • pinch of salt and sugar • 300 g walnuts • 120 g granulated sugar • 80 g milk • 10 g raisins • pinch of cinnamon • ground orange skin • 300 g dark chocolate • 300 g heavy cream • 50 g rum

Method

Mix the eggs, the milk, the sugar and the salt with a whisker then add the flour and whisk it until completely smooth. Add the seltzer water, a little at the time, until the batter is the consistency of thin sour cream. Set aside to rest for 30 minutes.

Brush a 200 mm frying pan with oil and heat over medium-high heat. Pour about ⅓ cup of batter into the pan and tilt the pan to cover it with the batter. Cook for 20 seconds, turn the crêpe over for 20 seconds until set.

Fry the walnuts in a pan, grind half of them, and chop the other half finely. Mix the other ingredients in a pan, bring them to the boil and stir the walnuts into it.

Heat the heavy cream, add the dark chocolate and carefully melt it. (Make sure it does not get to the boil.) Stir it smoothly and add the rum.

Fill the crêpes with the filling and fold them into triangle shape.

Top it with the chocolate sauce and sprinkle it with icing sugar.

♈ Recommended wine

Tokaji Aszú 6 puttonyos 1993 – Gundel Cellar
The famous dessert of Károly Gundel which is
dominated by the flavoured walnut cream and the
real chocolate. An excellent 6 Puttonyos Aszú
has to mature for 20 years to fulfil the task of
accompanying our speciality with its fruity, walnut,
caramel and sweet spicy aromas.

60 Baked Prune Pancakes

One of the recipes from the new age of our restaurant. Simple, but with a little twist which makes it to stand out.

Serves 8

8 pancakes (see p. 162) • **250 ml sour cream** • **4 egg yolks** • **4 egg whites** • **1 stick of vanilla** • **50 g sugar** • **150 g prunes** • **150 g plum jam** • **40 ml rum**

Method

First, soak the prunes in rum at room temperature for approx. 3 hours. Beat the egg yolks with half of the sugar, and the egg whites with the other half.

Chop the prunes into small pieces and mix half of the jam in. Carve the inside of the vanilla stick out and add it to half of the sour cream. Mix the beaten egg yolks into the sour cream gently, and keep stirring until smooth. Next, add the beaten egg whites to the mixture.

Fill the pancakes with the prunes and jam and roll them up. Place the filled pancakes in layers in an oven-proof dish and pour the sour cream and eggs over them. Bake for 50 minutes at approx 95 degrees Celsius.

Boil the remaining jam with rum, and then mix it with the rest of the sour cream.

Y **Recommended wine**

Szekszárdi Néró 2012 (sweet) – Gábor Merfelsz
The dessert is dominated by the deep flavour
tones of the plums. The wine is a special, hand
made 'micro' one which features the deep
aromas of the plums too.

61 Somlói Sponge Cake

The classic dessert is one of the restaurant's very own creation. It was named after the maker, who was a waiter in Gundel in those days.

Serves 4

1 dl rum • 80 g raisins • 100 g walnuts (without the shell) • for the sponge cake: 8 eggs • 160 g sugar • 160 g flour • 20 g cocoa powder • for the yellow cream: 0.5 litre milk • 1 vanilla stick • 4 eggs • 100 g sugar • 30 g flour • for the syrup: 200 g sugar • 3 dl water • orange peel, lemon peel • 20 g cocoa powder • 300 g sweet cream • 3 portions of chocolate sauce

Method

On the previous day soak the raisins in rum and grind the walnuts. To make the sponge cake whisk the egg whites with slowly added sugar into hard foam, then add the egg yolks and the flour. Divide the material into three parts: mix one third with the walnuts, one third with 20 g cocoa powder and the last third remains unflavoured. Bake the three cakes (about 10 mm high) in medium hot oven.

For the yellow cream boil the milk with the vanilla, add the egg yolks, sugar, flour and the egg white foam and mix it carefully.

For the syrup boil the sugar in the water with a little orange and lemon peel, and when it cools down add the rum.

When putting the Somlói cake together start with the walnut-flavoured sponge cake, sprinkle it with one third of the syrup, the walnuts and the raisins, then spread one third of the yellow cream on top. Place the cocoa-flavoured sponge cake layer on it, and repeat the procedure. Finally place the unflavoured sponge cake layer on top and do the same. To serve it in the classic style spread the leftover yellow cream on top and sprinkle it with cocoa powder. When finished, put it into the fridge for a few hours. After that, scoop 'noodles' out of it with a tablespoon, pile them up on a plate, cover it with sweet cream and pour chocolate sauce on top before serving.

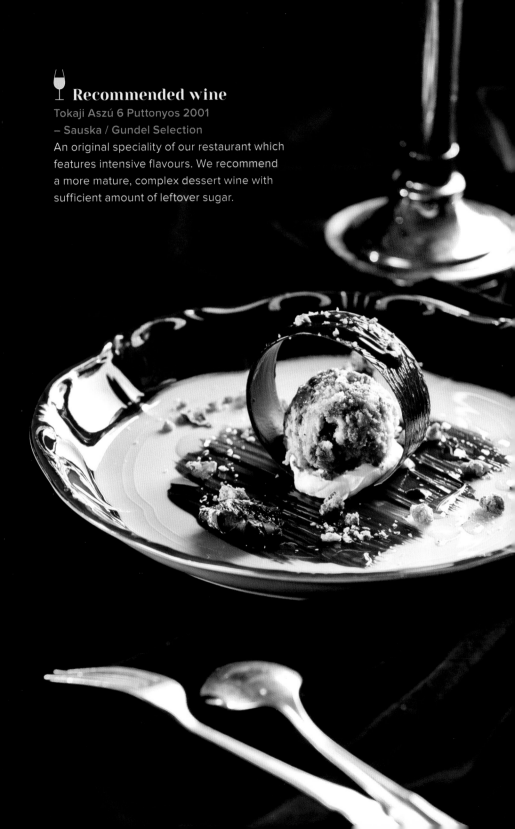

♀ Recommended wine

Tokaji Aszú 6 Puttonyos 2001
– Sauska / Gundel Selection

An original speciality of our restaurant which
features intensive flavours. We recommend
a more mature, complex dessert wine with
sufficient amount of leftover sugar.

62 Gundel's Chocolate Mousse

One of our lightest desserts, which is very popular amongst the ladies. It can be really attractive if made from three different types of chocolates.

Approx. 20 servings

4 egg yolks· 1 egg · 100 g caster sugar · 30 g water · 300 g dark chocolate · 500 g whipped cream

Method

Start whisking the whole egg with the egg yolks. Prepare syrup using the sugar and water and boil to 117 degrees Celsius (if you do not have a thermometer, make a loop using a piece of thin wire and dip it into the syrup. The syrup is hot enough when you can blow bubbles). Pour the sugar syrup onto the whisked eggs and carry on beating until cool. Melt the chocolate over steam and mix it all with the whipped cream.

Tip: if you substitute the 300 g dark chocolate with $1/3$ dark chocolate, $1/3$ milk chocolate and $1/3$ white chocolate, you will have 3 different types of mousse.

Let it settle in the fridge, and serve when solidified.

♟ Recommended wine

Calem LBW Portói 2004
Surprisingly sweet chocolate mousse.
We can choose a wine from further west,
where the making of strong, special,
sweet red wines has a long tradition.

63 Gundel Parfait

Originally, it was called Gellért Parfait, because the dish was born in Hotel Gellért where Károly Gundel worked for 25 years.

Serves 4

100 ml cream • **120 g blueberry jam** • **2 egg yolks** • **1 egg** • **40 g icing sugar** • **15 ml water** • Vanilla cream: **150 ml milk** • half a vanilla stick • **2 egg yolks** • **60 g icing sugar** • Hot cherry sauce: **60 g icing sugar** • **40 ml water** • **200 g cherries sprinkled with brandy** • Chocolate sauce: **120 g chocolate, 52% cocoa content** • **50 ml cream**

Method

Start whisking the whole egg with the egg yolks. Prepare syrup using the sugar and water and boil to 117 degrees Celsius (if you do not have a thermometer, make a loop using a piece of thin wire and dip it into the syrup. The syrup is hot enough when you can blow bubbles). Pour the sugar syrup into the whisked eggs and continue beating until cool. Use a sieve to separate the blueberry jam and add the liquid part to the whipped cream, then mix it with the whisked eggs and syrup. Pour the resulting mixture into molds and place them into the freezer.

To make vanilla cream: boil the milk with the sugar and vanilla stick, then removing it from the heat, add the egg yolk.

Cherry sauce: boil all the ingredients in a pot until half the water has evaporated and the sauce begins to thicken. Remove from the heat to add the brandy.

For the chocolate sauce, start heating the cream in a pot and melt the chocolate in it, stirring continuously. Make sure the cream does not burn and does not boil either.

Remove the parfait from the freezer, pour chocolate sauce over it, then make a dent in the middle and pour vanilla sauce into it. Cover in cherry sauce and serve.

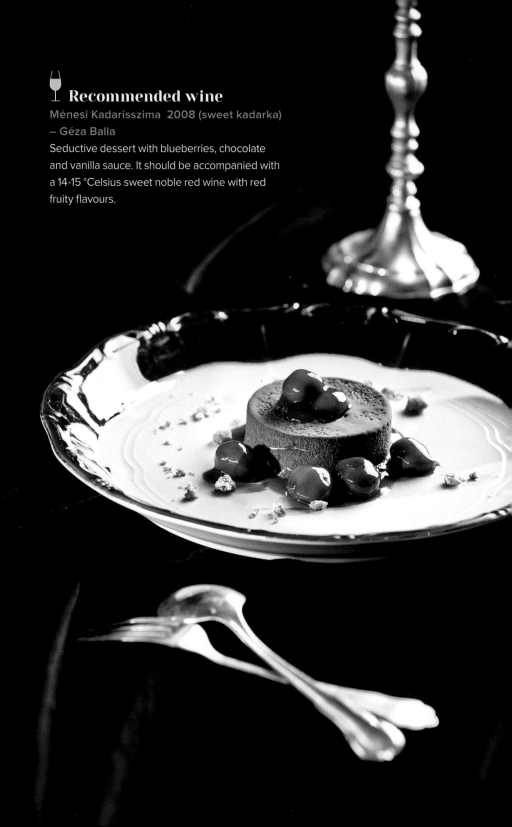

🍷 Recommended wine

Ménesi Kadarisszima 2008 (sweet kadarka)
– Géza Balla
Seductive dessert with blueberries, chocolate
and vanilla sauce. It should be accompanied with
a 14-15 °Celsius sweet noble red wine with red
fruity flavours.

64 Chocolate Parfait with Goat Cheese

The sweet and salty goat cheese makes the chocolate flavours more characteristic and excitingly spicy.

Serves 6

4 egg yolks • 1 egg • 100 g caster sugar • 30 g water • 300 g dark chocolate • 500 g whipped cream • 100 g goat cheese • Salty caramel sauce: 200 ml cream • 200 g sugar

Method

Make parfait base (see below). If you wish to flavour the parfait, you can add brittle, Nescafe, candied orange peel or even chilli. For a fruity flavour, use white chocolate instead of dark (in this case we recommend 400 g chocolate) and add puréed fruit to the parfait. If you are making a mousse, follow the same recipe - just use the refrigerator instead of the freezer for cooling.

Beat the whole egg and egg yolks with a mixer. Meanwhile, prepare syrup using the sugar and water and boil to 117 degrees Celsius (if you do not have a thermometer, make a loop using a piece of thin wire and dip it into the syrup. The syrup is hot enough when you can blow bubbles). Add the sugar syrup to the whipped eggs and continue beating until cool.

Melt the chocolate over steam. Next, mix with whipped cream and the beaten eggs with it. Crumble the goat cheese and add to the mixture. Pour into silicon moulds and freeze.

For serving, prepare a salty caramel sauce. Caramelise the sugar on high heat in a pan, and add an equal amount of cream. It is better to heat the cream separately before adding it to the caramel, in order to avoid spattering. Add a pinch of salt and cook until smooth.

Recommended wine

Hungária Rosé Champagne (semi dry)
Interesting marriage of sweetness and salty
caramel sauce. The choice is a sweet bubbly drink
to guide us to the next course.

65 Strawberries with Meringue and Tokaji Wine

Although it looks complicated to prepare, it is actually a really simple dessert with clear-out flavours.

Serves 4

400 g fresh strawberries • 3 egg whites • 175 g sugar • 5 g brown sugar • 200 g butter pastry • 150 ml cream (30%) • 200 ml Tokaji wine

Method

To make meringues: preheat the oven to 130 degrees. Place the egg whites into a metal bowl and whisk until soft. Start adding sugar, one spoonful at a time. Continue beating until the egg whites are hard and shiny. Line a baking tray with baking paper and use a tablespoon to form 6 mounds from the whisked eggs, placing them into the pan.

Bake for 75 minutes for soft-centred meringues of 90 minutes for dry meringues. When the time is up, switch the oven off but do not take the meringues out. Leave them inside the oven for 4 hours, until completely dry.

Whip the cream and place it in the fridge (always use cold cream for whipping, warm cream does not whip). Roll the butter pastry till 3 mm thin, sprinkle brown sugar on top and place in the oven, preheated to 180 degrees Celsius for approx. 12 minutes (always make sure butter pastry is cold when putting it into the oven).

Heat up a pan for the Tokaji wine, and when it is warm, pour the wine in slowly, then reduce it to $^2/_3$ of the quantity.

🍷 Recommended wine

Tahitótfalui Eperbor (sweet) 2012 – Kallós Cellar
Popular fruity dessert with noble Tokaji wine.
Apart from the obvious Tokaji Aszú (which it is
made with) we can try a special, sweet
strawberry wine to surprise our taste buds.

66 Chocolate and Raspberry Cake

An emblematic dessert of the modern restaurant. More variations feature on the menu of the restaurant and our patisserie as well.

12 pieces

150 g marzipan • 2 eggs • 4 egg yolks • 10 g cooking oil • 90 g dark chocolate • 15 g flour • 30 g cocoa powder • 300 g raspberry jam • 200 g chocolate ganache (see p. 188) • 300 g raspberry jam • Chocolate mousse: 2 egg yolks • 1 egg • 20 g caster sugar • 30 g water • 75 g dark chocolate • 150 g whipped cream

Method

For the cake base, knead the marzipan with oil. Add the whole eggs and egg yolks and beat it all together in a fast spinning blender. Stir the melted chocolate into the blend until smooth, taking care not to break the whisked eggs. Sprinkle the flour mixed with cocoa powder into the mixture. Spread 3 circular sheets of dough (18 cm in diameter) onto some baking paper and bake at 180 degrees for 8-10 minutes.

For the chocolate mousse beat the egg with the egg yolks and make syrup from the water and sugar (see p. 191). Pour the sugar syrup into the beaten eggs and continue beating until cold. Melt the chocolate over steam and mix all the ingredients with whipped cream.

For assembling the cake, layer the 3 circular sheets of dough with raspberry jam and spread chocolate mousse on the top layer. Let the cake cool in the fridge until the chocolate mousse solidifies. When it is done, cover the top of the cake in chocolate ganache (see p. 188).

♀ Recommended wine

Brill Málnapálinka 2011

A less sweet dessert with raspberries
and the finely bitter taste of black chocolate.
I recommend the drink which proved to be
really successful amongst our guests during
my working years.

67 Chocolate Napoleon

A newer version of the classic French creamy cake with a little twist: chocolate. The key to the perfect result is timing.

Serves 6

250 g puff pastry • **500 g milk** • **120 g caster sugar** • **60 g flour** • **4 eggs** • **1 vanilla stick** • **200 g cream** • **40 g dark chocolate** • for the chocolate coated sheet of pastry: **100 g dark chocolate** • **spoonful of cooking oil**

Method

Divide the 250 g puff pastry into two equal parts and roll to 3-4 mm. Pierce several times with a fork and bake in the oven (preheated to 210 degrees Celsius) until golden brown. When it has cooled, place a rectangular cake mold on one of the sheets of pastry and cut around the edges.

Mix the flour and egg yolk with a little milk until smooth. Boil the remaining milk with half of the sugar and the vanilla stick, then add the flour and egg yolks and continue cooking. Meanwhile, beat the egg whites with the remaining sugar till medium hard and fold into the hot cream gently, without breaking it. Pour the mixture into the prepared tin and let it cool.

Melt 40 g dark chocolate over steam. When it has cooled a little, but is not completely cold yet, add the half-whipped cream and spread over the pastry. Let it to cool. Coat the other sheet of pastry in melted dark chocolate mixed with a spoonful of cooking oil. Place the chocolate coated pastry on top of the bottom sheet, which is topped with cream. When it has hardened, remove the mold and serve.

Recommended wine

Szekszárdi Cabernet Sauvignon 2009
– Gábor Németh
A less sweet dessert with the intensive tastes
of good quality chocolate. Surprisingly a dry,
not too acidic, mature wine is our choice with
sweet tannins and stronger in alcohol.

68 Chocolate Lava (Soufflé)

A restaurant cannot be a real one without a soufflé.
According to the season we have walnut, hazelnut and
Grand Marnier soufflés, but the chocolate is a real classic.

Serves 6

5 eggs • 40 g flour • 80 g icing sugar • 80 g butter • 120 g dark
chocolate • strawberry

Method

Melt the chocolate with the butter and stir in the other ingredients until
smooth. Pour the mixture into heatproof cups or molds and bake in
the oven at 160 degrees Celsius for 8 minutes, until ready.
Serve with any kind of fresh seasonal fruits, strawberry for instance.

🍷 Recommended wine

Kadarisszima 2008 – Géza Balla
Chocolate dream with fresh strawberries.
We recommend again this special, sweet
red wine before from Aradhegyalja.

69 Gundel Chocolate and Marzipan Cake

This cake could be called 'Take a piece of Gundel with you', because it can be bought in the restaurant, the patisserie and in the boutique as well.

12 slices

4 eggs • 80 g caster sugar • 40 g dark chocolate, min. 50% • 35 g flour • 35 g walnuts • 10 g almonds • 50 g marzipan • Chocolate cream: 300 g dark chocolate, min. 50% • 300 ml cream • Covering chocolate: 150 g dark chocolate, min. 50% • 20 ml rapeseed oil

Method

First, melt the chocolate over steam. Chop the walnuts and the almonds. Whisk the egg yolk with half of the sugar and mix it with the melted chocolate. Meanwhile, beat the egg whites with the remaining sugar and gently mix them with the egg yolks and chocolate. While mixing, sprinkle the oily nuts with flour in as well. Be careful not to break the whisked eggs. Pour the cake mix into a 18 cm diameter circular mold and bake in the oven at 160 degrees Celsius for approx. 30 minutes. When the cake has cooled, cut it horizontally into 3 equal parts.

Melt the chocolate over steam and then stir in the hot (but not boiled!) cream until smooth. Let it cool at room temperature, then whisk.

Roll the marzipan to a circular shape 18 cm diameter. Layer the cake, filling it with chocolate cream. Place the layer of marzipan on top of the first layer of cream. When finished, spread the remaining chocolate cream over the top and sides of the cake and let it solidify. Finally, cover in melted dark chocolate: see below.

Melt the chocolate over steam and add all the oil. Spread over the cake evenly using a flat knife. Keep in the fridge until it solidifies.

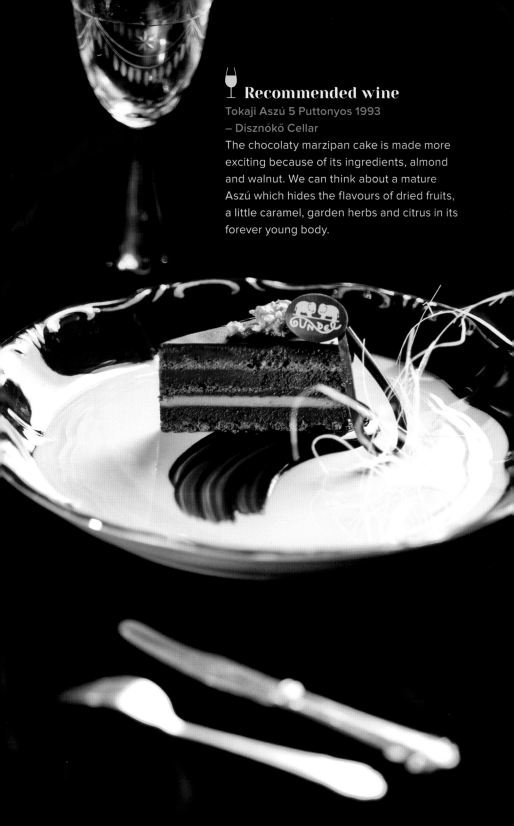

♜ Recommended wine

Tokaji Aszú 5 Puttonyos 1993
– Disznókő Cellar

The chocolaty marzipan cake is made more exciting because of its ingredients, almond and walnut. We can think about a mature Aszú which hides the flavours of dried fruits, a little caramel, garden herbs and citrus in its forever young body.

70 Chocolate and Nut Slice

One of our newer desserts. The chef's favourite is chocolate with nuts – he created this cake to acquire the same taste.

12 slices, serves 6

80 g flour • 80 g caster sugar • 80 g nuts, finely ground • 80 g milk • 40 g butter • 2 eggs • a pinch of salt • 250 g dark chocolate • 220 g cream

Method

First, beat the butter with half of the sugar and the eggs, then add milk, stir and set aside. Next, use the remaining sugar to beat the egg whites with, then mix the egg whites gently into the buttery part, while sprinkling the ground nuts and flour in, too. (Tip: if very finely ground nuts are available, you can use them instead of flour as well, resulting in a gluten free cake).

Place the mixture into a circular cake mold and bake at 160 degrees Celsius for approx. 25-30 minutes.

For the ganache cream (see p. 188) melt the chocolate over steam. Add the warmed up (but not boiled) cream and stir until smooth.
Tip: you can make your cake even more unique if you splash sugar syrup flavoured with liqueur (eg. Grand Marnier) on the pastry.

When the cake has cooled, pour the Ganache cream over it smoothly. Sprinkle chopped roast nuts on top.

Slice the cake when the cream on top has solidified.

♀ Recommended wine

Tokaji Szamorodni Sweet 2008
– Barta Cellar
Chocolate dessert served with roasted
nuts and orange liqueur. The mature
wine has fruity citrus flavours, enough
sweetness and creamy texture to provide
perfect harmony.

Measures and Abbreviations

1 tablespoon • a tablespoon of 15 ml volume
The word 'tablespoon' in the recipes always means level
(but loose, not tightly packed) spoonful, unless otherwise indicated.

1 teaspoon • a teaspoon of 5 ml volume
½ teaspoon • a teaspoon of 2 ml volume
¼ teaspoon • a teaspoon of 1 ml volume
The word 'teaspoon' in the recipes always means a level
(but loose, not tightly packed) spoonful, unless otherwise indicated.

1 cup • a cup of 250 ml volume
½ cup • a cup of 125 ml volume
⅓ cup • a cup of 80 ml volume
¼ cup • a cup of 60 ml volume
⅛ cup • a cup of 30 ml volume
The word 'cup' in the recipes always means a level
(but loose, not tightly packed) cupful, unless otherwise indicated.

Dry ingredients should be measured in cups designed for dry measuring so that they can be leveled with the back of a knife or small spatula.

Liquid ingredients should be measured in liquid measure cups.

Gundel Kitchen Guide

Bechamel or white sauce
2 tablespoons butter • 2 tablespoons flour • 0.5 l milk

Boil the milk and put it aside. Heat up the butter, mix in the flour and slowly grill it on low heat. Mix in the hot milk in small amounts, stirring constantly. When ready, add salt and pepper according to taste.

Beurre de Homard
250 g crayfish or crab or lobster (with the shell and chitterlings) • 250 g butter (not salty)

Crash the crayfish finely in a mortar. Place it in a pan with the butter, and cook until the buttermilk boils and evaporates. Sieve it and put it in a cool dry place until serving or using.

Beurre manié
Mix of the same amount of melted butter and white flour.

Blanching
Procedure used mostly as pre-cooking or conserving vegetables and fruits: put ingredients into a lot of boiling, hot water, and then cool it under cold water immediately.
Blanched fruits and vegetables keep their original flavours, stay crispy and keep their colours nice. (Adding a little lemon juice into the water, they would look even fresher.)

Brining

A pickling method that preceeds cooking. Add equal parts sugar and salt to cold water (50 g sugar and 50 g salt to 1000 ml water) to make souse. Place the souse into a deep dish or container and soak the meat into it for 6-12 hours. This is the necessary time for the brining method – the exact time depends on the size of the meat. Naturally, a large turkey will take longer than a broiler chicken, and a big roast longer than a thin slice of meat. The pickling makes the meat juicier as it hydrates the cells and the muscle tissue before cooking. The cells go through osmosis and as they are hydrated, the drying effect of cooking will only remove the extra water added during brining. Osmosis takes place because the salt concentration in the souse is higher than the salt concentration in the cells; however, the cells have a higher concentration of other substances. The density of the two substances is different – osmosis is the method leading to the equalisation of density. This stops the meat from drying out. There are 4 effects of the brining method:
- The meat comes into contact with the seasonings not only on the surface but also on the inside
- The meat takes on an extra 10-15% of its weight in water
- The high salt concentration in the cells reduces the chance of any bacteria surviving, so it is a good way to increase hygiene and food safety
- The meat's weight is not reduced during cooking

Brown sauce

10 ml rapeseed oil • 30 g onions chopped into 20 mm pieces • 30 g carrots chopped into 20 mm pieces • 30 g root parsley chopped into 20 mm pieces • 30 g celery chopped into 20 mm pieces • 1000 ml brown veal stock • 30 g wholemeal flour (baked in a 160 degree Celsius oven for approx. 12 minutes)

Use a large pot to fry the onions and the vegetables in oil until they are nicely browned. Add 1000 ml brown veal stock. Add the wholemeal flour to the sauce gradually, then simmer slowly, stirring continuously, for 2 hours. Remove any froth or grease from the top, and then strain.

Brown veal stock

2000 g veal bones or trimmings • 3000 ml water • 20 g onion chopped into 15 mm pieces • 20 g celery chopped into 15 mm pieces • 30 g carrots chopped into 15 mm pieces • 30 g root parsley chopped into 15 mm pieces

First, roast the bones until brown in a 200 degree Celsius oven. Next, place the bones into 3000 ml cold water and start cooking. Bring to the boil once, then simmer slowly for 6 hours. Meanwhile, brown the vegetables in a dry, hot pan, and add them to the sauce halfway through the cooking process. While the sauce is simmering, make sure to keep removing the froth and grease from the top continuously.

Brunoise

Means diced finely, 2 × 2 mm or 3 × 3 mm pieces.

Butter pastry

250 g flour • 250 g butter • 3 g salt • 5 ml vinegar (10%) • 125 ml cold water
First, knead 200 g butter with 50 g flour, then form a 2 cm thick rectangle from the mixture and place into the refrigerator. For the dough, dissolve the salt in cold water. Add the vinegar. Crumble the remaining flour with the remaining butter and then mix it with the cold salt and vinegar water. Knead the dough until the

surface is smooth and velvety. Form a bun shape from it and let it rest for 20-25 minutes. Roll the dough on a floury surface to make a cross shape, then place the butter mix into the middle. Fold the dough so that it covers the butter from all sides, then roll into a 5 mm thick rectangle. Next comes the folding process. Folding: Fold a third of the pastry from the right hand side into the middle, then repeat from the left hand side to make three layers (single folding). Turn the dough 90 degrees, then roll the right hand side to a 5 mm thick rectangle, and fold into the middle. Repeat with the left hand side. Finally, fold the whole sheet in half one more time (double folding) Let the dough rest in the refrigerator for 30 minutes. Repeat the folding process 2 more times, including the resting period, too.

Cherry sauce
500 g fresh cherries • 100 g butter • 50 g sugar • 100 ml red wine

Stone the cherries, then melt sugar in a frying pan until it is lightly caramellised. Pour the stoned cherries into the sugar with a quick movement. After browning the cherries for one minute, start adding the red wine in gradually, until it is all used up. Bring to the boil, then take the sauce off the heat and let it cool. When it has cooled, mix the butter in. Serve at room temperature and take care not to make more sauce than what will be consumed.

Chocolate coated cake
Enough to coat a 10-12 slice cake
250 g good quality dark chocolate • 10% volume rapeseed oil

Melt the chocolate over steam, stirring continuously. Gradually add the oil in to make the chocolate spreadable. Place the cake on a tray, on a plate turned upside down. Make sure the cake is not too cold, as this would cause the coating to solidify too quickly, not leaving enough time for spreading. Spread the chocolate coating evenly on the cake, taking care to leave enough to cover the sides, too.

Chocolate ganache
250 g good quality dark chocolate • 220 g cream

Melt the chocolate over steam, then pour the heated (but not boiled) cream into it and stir until smooth. When it has cooled, it can even be served on its own.

Chocolate sauce
350 g good quality dark chocolate • 300 g cream • 50 g rum

Start heating the cream, then add the chocolate and melt it, but do not let it boil. Stir until smooth and add the rum. The chocolate sauce is now ready to serve.

Clarifying the broth
The way to do this is to turn the heat down and mix the egg whites in, while stirring continuously with a whisk. Next, bring to the boil again, and then let it cool and strain the broth. When straining, make sure not to pour the broth, but to use a ladle.

Cleaning butter
Butter can either be cleaned by boiling, or heat treating below boiling point. For boiling, place the butter in a pan and heat it, stirring continuously. Bring it to a boiling point until the buttermilk precipitates and the butter is fried. Cool and then strain to separate the buttermilk. For heat treating below boiling point, place the

butter in a water bath and start heating slowly. When the butter has melted, keep heating it at a steady temperature so the buttermilk separates from the fat content. Following this, the fat can be removed and the buttermilk used to thicken soups or sauces.

Demi-glace sauce
3 cups of brown veal stock • 3 cups of brown sauce • 3 g salt

Use a 1 liter pot to boil the brown veal stock slowly, reducing it to one third. Add 3 cups of brown sauce. Simmer gently for 1 hour. Season with salt and then strain before serving.

Dumplings with butter
Beat the egg yolks with butter. Add the egg whites, then salt and flour. Use a spoon to form small dumplings and throw them into the boiling water. When the dumplings rise to the top, strain them.

Fish stock
1000 g fish bones • 4 grains of black pepper, whole • 30 g celery roots, chopped into 20 mm pieces • 30 g root parsley, chopped into 20 mm pieces • 30 g leeks, chopped into 20 mm pieces • 1500 ml water

Use a large pot to start boiling the fish bones with the vegetables and black pepper in 1500 ml water. Boil for 10 minutes, then take it off the heat and let it cool slowly for approx. 2 hours. Use a sieve or a cloth to strain the stock when it has cooled.

Glazing
Before serving lubricate the meat in its own juice, which makes its surface look shinier. This way the meat does not loose its colour.

Home-made bread, Gundel style
Makes 900 g bread: 630 g flour • 440 g water • 20 g salt • 10 g yeast • 20 g olive oil

Use a blender to mix the flour and water: blend for 2 minutes on the slow setting and then on fast setting for 7 minutes until smooth. Set aside for 30 minutes. Blend the following into the mixture, one by one: 20 g salt for 3 minutes on fast setting, 10 g yeast for 5 minutes on medium setting, 20 g olive oil for 8 minutes on slow setting. In order to get the right consistency, it is very important to follow the given order, adding the ingredients in one by one.
Knead the dough, cover with foil and let it rest for 1 day. Next day, form the bread (eg. Baguette-shaped). Let it rise for 30 minutes and then bake in a steamy oven at 190 degrees Celsius for 8 minutes. After this, let the steam out and bake the bread in the dry oven for a further 8 minutes.
As soon as you take the bread out of the oven, spread a little water over the surface.

Hominy
For firm hominy (to grill or batter after cooling): 100 g corn flour and four times as much water. For soft hominy: 100 g corn flour and five times as much water

Add the corn flour slowly to simmering water, stirring continuously. Cook for 3-4 minutes, then put it on low heat and continue cooking until the grains of corn flour are soft. Only add salt when the hominy is cooked. The better quality corn flour we use, the more delicious it will be. Hominy can also be cooked in milk or chicken stock. Butter and cheese can optionally be added.

Hungarian dumplings
100 g flour • 1 egg • 2 g salt • a few drops of water, if necessary

Knead the ingredients to make a firm dough.
Form approx. 3 mm dumplings with your thumb and forefinger and place them on a plate that has been sprinkled with flour. Cook in boiling water or soup for at least 15 minutes.
If you cannot use all the dumplings up, they can be dried in order to preserve them for another occasion. When you are reusing the dried dumplings, cook them for 20 minutes or until they are soft.

Lining the mold
Pour the fish jelly into the cooled molds until full, then dip them quickly into salted ice (or put them into the freezer) so that a sufficient layer of jelly freezes onto the insides of the mold. Pour the rest of the jelly out of the mold.

Marinating
Marinating is a procedure to flavour food or to change its texture without heat treating. It can be done in salt, sugar, citrus juices or any combination of these with spices. Marinating in grease and oil is not possible!

Meat stock
Meat stock can be prepared from any type of meat. There is no exact recipe, but here are a few important things to remember. Stock should not be seasoned either with salt or sugar, or any other strong spices. Only use a small amount of vegetables to give it flavour. The amount of water used should be 3 times the volume of the meat. After bringing the stock to the boil, simmer slowly on a low heat so that the flavour has time to brew. It should take approx. 3-4 hours. After cooking, strain the stock.

Reducing
Boiling until half of the original liquid evaporates.

Sauce Supreme
30 g butter • 30 g white flour • 500 ml chicken stock • 1 egg yolk • 250 ml cream • 25 g cold butter

Make chicken velouté sauce. Heat butter in a pan, bring it to a boiling point and then add flour. When the butter is frothing with the flour, add all the chicken stock. Simmer for at least 30 minutes. Next, add the egg yolk mixed with cream but do not boil. Finally, stir the cold butter in quickly – this is how to make Sauce Supreme from Veolute sauce.

„Serviette dumplings"
For 4 × 750 g rolls: 1600 g bread soaked in water (just enough water to cover it) • 800 g diced white bread, toasted in a 160 degree Celsius oven for 10 mins • 4 eggs, beaten • 100 g melted duck fat • 400 g onions, chopped finely and fried • 14 g salt • 4 g freshly ground white pepper • 100 g parsley, chopped finely

First, squeeze the water out of the soaked bread. Mix the bread with the eggs, duck fat, fried onion, salt, pepper and chopped parsley, then add the toasted bread croutons and divide into 4 equal parts. Put a portion of the bread mix on a clean dish cloth and wrap around to make a 60 mm diameter cylinder shape. Tie both ends tightly. Next, boil water in a deep baking tray, adding 10 g salt. When the water comes to the boil, cook the dumpling rolls in it, 2 at a time. Make sure the water is just simmering gently, not boiling. When the dumplings are cooked, cool down and slice. Before serving, brown both sides in duck fat.

Slow cooking (confit)

Cooking slowly, under boiling temperature in a lot of fat (clean butter, fat or good quality olive oil).

Sour cherry confit (in red wine syrup)

1000 ml red wine • 400 g sugar • 500 g fresh, stoned sour cherries • 1 vanilla stick

Brown sugar in a dry pan. When the sugar turns golden brown, start adding the red wine to it gradually. When all the wine has been added, reduce to a third of the original volume. Add the stoned sour cherries to the red wine syrup and cook very slowly on a low heat, until the cherries harden. (The sugary syrup extracts liquid from the cherries, so their texture changes from soft to hard).

Sugar syrup

Take equal volumes of water and sugar and bring to the boil. Continue boiling for 5 minutes. Can be used either hot or cold.

Vegetable broth

500 g diced mixed vegetables • 1,5 l water

Place the vegetables into a suitable size pot and pour the water on top. Boil it and let it boil for another 5 minutes. Let it ccol down, sieve it and store it in a ccol dry place.

Water bath (Bain-marie)

This is a gentle cooking procedure where the dish placed into the water is not subjected to too much heat. Take a large pot and a smaller dish that fits into it comfortably. Fill the large one with water and place the smaller one inside. Heat the large pot on the cooker, warming up the smaller dish in it. This method is good not only for cooking, but also keeping food hot until serving.

To choose the perfect wine...

...there are basic rules which we should comply. Naturally it is important to follow the personal taste but this can be fine tuned in an exciting way. To create the food-wine harmony we should take into consideration the richness, the complexity, the basic flavours, the significant aromas, the spiciness, the colours, the freshness, the occasion and the season, which all have an effect on the drinks and the dishes as well.
The year and the wines mentioned in the book change as time goes by, so we should consider that when choosing a wine.

The book was commissioned by the Gundel Restaurant
to celebrate the 130th anniversary of Károly Gundel's birth.

Recipes
Gábor Merczi
Gundel Restaurant – Executive Chef

Photo
Pixeltaster – Árpád Pintér

Translation
Júlia Gárdos, Eszter Cooper

Editor
Ági Nimila

Graphic Design, Image Processing
Annamária Csermák

Head of Production
Bálint Ördögh

Project Manager
Jolanta Szuba

All Rights Reserved

ISBN 978-963-09-7647-3

© Kossuth Publishing 2013

Publisher
András Sándor Kocsis
Managing Director of Kossuth Publishing
The publishin house is a member of the Association
of Hungarian Book Publishers and Distributors founded in 1795.

Layouter
Katalin Csermák

Printed and bound by
Dürer Printing House in Gyula
Manager in charge
János Kovács CEO